Civil War
in
Kansas

"Everything disloyal, from a Shanghai rooster to a Durham cow, must be cleaned out." —Jim Lane

Civil War
in
Kansas

Roy Bird

Illustrated by Michael Almond

PELICAN PUBLISHING COMPANY
Gretna 2004

Library of Congress Cataloging-in-Publication Data

Bird, Roy, 1952-
  Civil War in Kansas / Roy Bird.
    p. cm.
Includes bibliographical references (p.   ) and index.
  ISBN 1-58980-164-4 (pbk. : alk. paper)
1. Kansas-History-Civil War, 1861-1865. I. Title.

  E508.B57 2004
  973.7'09781-dc22
  2003022465

Printed in the United States of America

Published by Pelican Publishing Company, Inc.
1000 Burmaster Street, Gretna, Louisiana 70053

To Kansas Civil War scholars and buffs

Contents

Preface

This chronicle of the involvement of Kansas and Kansans in the American Civil War follows the exploits of many people in one of the most trying times in American history. It is based on events, incidents, and daily activities both great and mundane as they were recorded by many historians and writers. The intent is to divulge what interesting things occurred involving Kansas in the Civil War; to bring together some of the many facts and stories of this fascinating era in a single volume; to paint a panorama of all aspects of the war that touched the state; and to present the information in an interesting and entertaining format.

Some historians claim that the Civil War started not on the traditionally accepted date of April 12, 1861, with the firing on Fort Sumter but in May 1854, with the passage of the Kansas-Nebraska Act. I concur. At the opposite end of the spectrum, others argue that the war came to a close with the surrender of Confederate Gen. Robert E. Lee to Union Gen. Ulysses S. Grant in April 1865 (that is, if the war was not over even earlier in Kansas). Yet, in fact, the last Confederate forces in the Trans-Mississippi West did not surrender until June 1865. And one famous Rebel cavalry officer with whom Kansans contended, Gen. Joseph O. Shelby, never surrendered but went to Mexico instead.

Regardless of the earliest and latest dates of the conflict, all Kansas Civil War academics and fans agree that the war itself had a tremendous impact on the state. The experience of the war left a lasting impression on the development of Kansas for the rest of the 19th century. This war solidified the population behind the Union and totally as Americans. Finally, the very nature of the unforgiving, no-holds-barred war—partly conventional, partly brutal guerrilla tactics—left an indelible imprint on the population of the state.

No book is the result of the efforts of only one person, regardless of the amount of work the author invests. And sometimes the results of a book are serendipitous. In the case of this book, the beginning was actually the submission of an entirely different manuscript. After a couple of looks at that submission, editor Nina Kooij suggested I undertake this project in Pelican's series. For her confidence, I thank her.

I would like to thank the many readers, Civil War buffs, and colleagues who have lent me encouragement. Of course, I am deeply indebted to the authors, living and dead, listed in this book's bibliography; they made this small tome possible.

Finally, my family deserves honorable mention. They have seen many sites, dodged stacks of books, and listened to unsolicited discourses on the Civil War or Kansas—more or less patiently—throughout their lives. For this they deserve my deepest gratitude.

Introduction

The Kansas-Nebraska Act, with its popular-sovereignty provision, made Kansas Territory a battleground. In reality, despite the bloodthirsty acts of hotheads among both proslavery "border ruffians" and "bushwhackers" and anti-slavery Free-Staters and "Jayhawkers," there was little actual violence during the territorial period. What bloodshed there was, including the killings by John Brown, caused Kansas to be known as "bleeding Kansas," and stirred passions that pushed Americans into the Civil War. It was during the Civil War that Kansas really bled.

The opening of Kansas Territory led to the first major settlement by white Americans. Southerners immigrated to the territory with a few slaves for political reasons as well as to protect their way of life; thousands of Northerners flooded the territory because they were morally opposed to slavery. Both sides hoped to provide enough voters in the territory to determine its fate, either a free state or a slave state.

But most of the new settlers who arrived in the territory between 1854 and 1861, when Kansas became a state, were from Ohio, Indiana, Illinois, and Kentucky. The primary reason for these settlers to come to Kansas Territory was to make new homes for themselves. As Kenneth S. Davis wrote in *Kansas: A Bicentennial History,* "they were driven by land-hunger, drawn by the promise of free land. The conscious purpose of making

Kansas free, though present and strong in most of them, was subordinate and incidental."

The acts of violence during the territorial period were inspired by politics, but they had little to do with territorial politics. The battles began in the autumn of 1855. Threats of violence had been made earlier, and occasional brawls made Kansas Territory a lively place in which to live. But on November 21, 1855, a proslave man, Franklin Coleman, shot and killed a Free-Stater, Charles Dow, over a land boundary dispute after the intrusion of Missouri border ruffians into the first Kansas election.

This precipitated the "Wakarusa War," as Free-Staters rushed to defend Lawrence, the largest city, their stronghold, and their headquarters along the Wakarusa River, from proslavery militia. For the next three years the rival sides clashed at such places as Hickory Point, Blackjack, in the streets of Topeka, at Pottawatomie Creek, Osawatomie, and on the banks of the Marais des Cygnes River.

Bleeding Kansas grew less bloody in 1858, and in 1859 a constitution was hammered out. It was based on the Ohio constitution, under which Kansas would enter the Union as a free state. Much of 1860 saw intense lobbying of Congress and the administration for the admission of the 34th state. Jubilation swept Kansans when President James Buchanan signed the statehood bill on January 29, 1861.

When war erupted, some Southern sympathizers fled to Missouri, Arkansas, and Texas. Early in the war, vengeance by Jayhawkers became ugly. Under the guise of Federal service, Kansans revisited the terror of the territorial struggle on the despised citizens of Missouri. Irregular tactics, murder, plunder, and burning were the order of the day. This in turn spawned renewed savage guerrilla retaliation by Missourians along the border. Communities and farms on either side of the state line were in smoking ruin.

In the first year of the war, President Abraham Lincoln called for 16,600 volunteers from Kansas, even though there were only about 30,000 of military age in the whole state. Nevertheless, 20,097 volunteered, or about two out of every three Kansas men old enough to serve. Of them, 8,498 were casualties. Records show that 2,080 African-Americans served in Kansas regiments, although the census indicates there were only 300 black males of military age in the state. Many were ex-slaves recruited in Missouri.

There were also about 3,500 American Indians in Kansas regiments. Some of the nastiest fights of the Civil War took place near Kansas—and Kansas soldiers took part in almost every one of them. This work will provide a glimpse of the impact of the war on the local population of Kansas as well as the role the state played in the War Between the States.

Civil War
in
Kansas

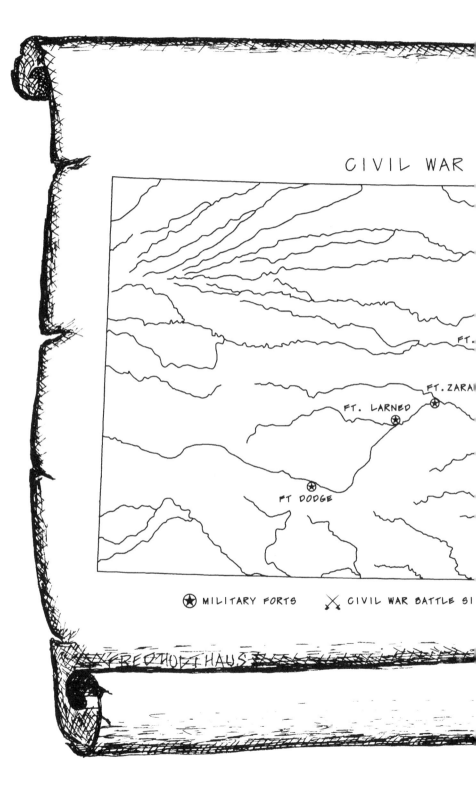

CIVIL WAR

FT.

FT. ZARA

FT. LARNED

FT DODGE

⊛ MILITARY FORTS   ✕ CIVIL WAR BATTLE SI

REQHOFFHAUS

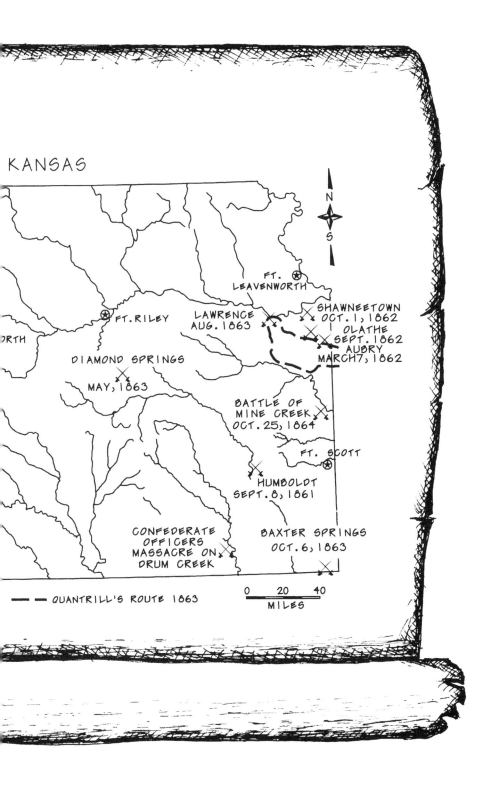

KANSAS

FT. LEAVENWORTH

FT. RILEY

LAWRENCE
AUG. 1863

SHAWNEETOWN
OCT. 1, 1862

OLATHE
SEPT. 1862

AUBRY
MARCH 7, 1862

DIAMOND SPRINGS
MAY, 1863

BATTLE OF
MINE CREEK
OCT. 25, 1864

FT. SCOTT

HUMBOLDT
SEPT. 8, 1861

CONFEDERATE
OFFICERS
MASSACRE ON
DRUM CREEK

BAXTER SPRINGS
OCT. 6, 1863

— — QUANTRILL'S ROUTE 1863

0   20   40
MILES

N
S

James H. Lane.

CHAPTER 1

"From a Shanghai Rooster to a Durham Cow": 1861-62

Kansas was only a little more than two months old when the United States entered its most tragic and violent decade in the spring of 1861. However, many historians justifiably argue that the Civil War actually started in the territorial strife of "bleeding Kansas." The new state came into being when seven Southern states seceded from the Union, and their senators and representatives departed from Congress. Without the slave state votes, the statehood bill passed easily.

When Kansans learned that President Buchanan had signed the bill admitting Kansas to the Union as a free state on January 29, 1861, they stood on corners in every town cheering, dancing in the streets, and singing patriotic songs. Cannons were fired and fireworks lighted to signal their joy. Newspaper editors waxed eloquent: "We are citizens of the United States once more—partners in 'Hail Columbia,' 'Yankee Doodle,' the stars and stripes, the Declaration of Independence, and the Fourth of July!" wrote one. Another added, "Hurrah for us, we ourselves! Hurrah for the New Star. And three times three again for the NEW STATE OF KANSAS!"

The mobilization and hardships of war were not unfamiliar to people in Kansas. Neither were other hardships, and they bred a hearty, self-reliant, determined population with which the Southern Confederacy would have to contend. Although the violence and bloodshed of "bleeding Kansas" had subsided by 1859, a new struggle began. The first marked drought in Kansas history started, and from June 1859 to November 1860, searing sun and dry winds withered crops and vegetation. There were only a few showers, not even enough to settle the dust, for a year and a half. Eastern states had sent clothing, seed, and other relief to aid some of those same people.

There were only ten towns in Kansas with more than 500 citizens. With a population of about 5,000, Leavenworth approached the status of a city. Lawrence and Atchison were distant competitors. Leavenworth garnered much local business from the garrison at Fort Leavenworth. The economic base of both Atchison and Leavenworth was trade from the Missouri River and freighting into the West.

Levees along the river boasted great warehouses storing goods from the East that arrived by steamboat. They were to be hauled further west along the network of military roads past Fort Riley in large, ox-drawn freight wagons, returning loaded with furs, hides, and other natural resources from the frontier.

The river towns were main stopovers for travelers because they could make connections between the steamboats and stagecoach lines that originated there. Further inland, Lawrence scorned the large number of saloons and houses of ill repute found in the river cities.

In January 1861, a series of blizzards helped break the drought. Lawrence was cut off from outside news because of heavy snows. The territorial legislature waited there where its members had met in session for word on the pending statehood bill and its signature by lame-duck President James Buchanan. They would be snowbound for more than two weeks. During the entire Civil War transportation and communications in Kansas were poor even in the best weather.

There were only a few miles of railroad tracks laid in 1860, at Elwood. Although there were attempts to establish steamboat traffic on the Kansas River, other waterways were unnavigable and described as "amphibious—half water and half mud."

Leavenworth was the only town with a telegraph connection with the East, and that was only because of the fort. News was relayed by messengers on horseback or by stagecoach. Indeed, on April 3, 1861, the Pony Express celebrated its first—and only—anniversary. It would go out of business by the fall of 1861. Mail was erratic at best—some pioneers were over sixty miles from the nearest post office. Once a week "a stage coach ran, or rather crawled" from Kansas City to Mound City.

The overland mail route from Atchison opened on January 26 after being closed by snow and mud for three weeks. The sorry state of roads created a strong desire among Kansans in the 1860s for railroads that was "matched only by their need for them." In 1861, Kansans in the interior were willing to promise virtually anything to railroad promoters to bring tracks to their towns. Since there were only those few miles of track laid before the close of the war, railroads did not have the impact that they had in the eastern theaters of war.

On the frontier, the Arapaho and Cheyenne Indian tribes ceded all their lands to the United States, except a tract between the Sand Fork of the Arkansas (Sand Creek) and the Purgatory River. This tract is in southeastern Colorado Territory—the Cheyenne and Arapaho gave up their claim to all of western Kansas.

The tract in Colorado Territory surrounded the Big Timbers—a large cottonwood grove on the Arkansas River—and Bent's Fort, the stockaded trading post of William Bent. Because the region was swept nearly free of buffalo—upon which the Plains Indians depended for food, clothing, and lodging—by the 1850s, Indians could not live on the tract year-round.

To find the animals they required for sustenance, the Cheyenne and Arapaho moved eastward onto the Kansas plains each spring. In February 1861, the tribes signed away, albeit unwittingly, their livelihood by ceding their claim to buffalo grounds in Kansas. It was the first step toward eventual hostile confrontation.

When word did reach towns along the roads, it did not take long to spread. One of the first things to mark a town that would grow was a weekly newspaper. And Leavenworth boasted the first daily paper, the *Daily Conservative,* whose premier issue appeared on January 28, the day before Kansas Day. The newspaper was owned by Daniel R. Anthony, brother of Susan B. Anthony and a violently radical abolitionist.

The success of the paper was due in part to its editorial stance on Kansas and partly to the editor that Anthony hired, Daniel Webster Wilder. Possessor of the Franklin Medal from Boston Latin School and the Bowdoin Gold Medal from Harvard, Wilder was a member of the Massachusetts bar. He had recently been run out of St. Joseph, Missouri, a city in an area of slaveholders' large farms and hemp plantations, because of his "incendiary" style of journalism.

He found a venue for his kind of incendiarism in the favorable atmosphere of Leavenworth and Kansas. Although there would soon be two more daily newspapers in Leavenworth, the *Daily Conservative* was the most influential abolitionist newspaper in Kansas, one that would shape the Kansas view of the Civil War for generations to come.

Since Leavenworth was the only place with direct telegraphic communications, and because Anthony had close ties to abolitionists who controlled the wires, the *Conservative* not only was the first to announce the news of statehood but also issued an extra on the event. Anthony himself rode more than thirty miles through the snow to Lawrence, where the territorial legislature was in session, announcing the momentus tidings in each hamlet as he passed through.

While citizens of the newest state celebrated, organized, and prepared for elections, tensions between the Union and the Confederacy increased. In March 1861, four more states seceded from the Union, joining the original seven, and the remaining loyal states braced for conflict. On the eve of war, Capt. Nathaniel Lyon was called from his post at Fort Riley to take command of Federal troops at the St. Louis, Missouri, arsenal. Lyon hastened eastward down the Kansas and the Missouri rivers to begin training the Missouri Home Guards, soldiers who would defend the arsenal against Missouri secessionists.

Lyon was ordered to replace Maj. Peter Hagner, who had refused to strengthen the arsenal's defense. Captain Lyon was an ardent Unionist soon to be appointed general with the task to hold Missouri for the Union. He was a redheaded staunch Democrat who, after watching the border ruffians from Missouri, opposed proslavery groups.

To do so, he used Kansas volunteer regiments. His assignment came a week too late for many Union supporters. On the day of President Abraham Lincoln's inauguration, secessionists raised the Missouri state flag and a crudely fashioned Stars and Bars over the St. Louis courthouse in plain sight of the arsenal.

At 3:30 A.M. on April 12, 1861, Confederate Gen. P.G.T. Beauregard ordered the first shots of the War Between the States at Fort Sumter. A hysterical wave of emotion swept across the country in the wake of the news. Public sentiment in Kansas became, in the words of a contemporary, "very strongly patriotic." Members of the brand-new, first state legislature were "in favor of rigid enforcement of the laws at all hazards," and newspapers across the state ran special editions to speak indignantly against the rebellion.

The actions of Kansans were as militant as the editors' words. Everywhere they rushed to organize militia or volunteer military companies and held drills. One of the first acts of the legislature after Kansas was admitted to the Union was to pass a militia law. But in southeast Kansas, Linn and Bourbon counties did not wait for the legislature to act. The two counties joined together in February to organize the first militia company of the new state, the Mound City Sharp's Rifle Guards. Charles R. Jennison was elected captain.

The people of Mound City petitioned Gov. Charles Robinson to support Free-State leader James Montgomery as

Gen. Nathaniel Lyon.

commander of the Southern Division of the new state militia, with Jennison as his second in command. The cautious and conservative Robinson was less impressed with their military talents than their hot- headed abolitionist tendencies. In Jennison's case, the militia captain also consorted with the seamiest side of society. Hoping to avoid renewing the border troubles of the days of "bleeding Kansas," Governor Robinson failed to act on the suggestion. The legislature also gave Governor Robinson authority to raise volunteer troops and issued bonds to help pay for those soldiers. The only crusade preached in Kansas was preservation of the Union and punishment of the "southern fanatics." In fact, the abolitionists and radical Republicans of Kansas such as Montgomery and Jennison were every bit as fanatical as the secessionists—not to mention more altruistic.

Some of the Southern sympathizers who had settled in Kansas were not particularly fanatic. They had come to Kansas for the same reason as the majority of early settlers during the territorial era—not because of civil partisan politics, but to claim land for new homes and new beginnings. Some of them chose to mind their own business and stick it out in Kansas. Others fled to more friendly areas in the South.

For instance, a number of families from Jackson County, Missouri, an area of strong proslavery sentiments, pioneered near the village of Brownville, later Auburn, Kansas. It might even have been possible that one or two of these families brought a slave with them, although this was merely rumored, never proven. Yet when the Union militia of the area was called out during the war, the names of these Southern sympathizers appeared on the roster. The reason given was that they were defending their homes.

By the same token, one Southern family that had homesteaded in Jefferson County feared their Unionist neighbors and so fled the state, going first to Arkansas and later, when the war followed them to that Confederate state, to Tennessee. They returned to Jefferson County in 1867, two years after the war ended.

And in the first major battle of the Civil War at Wilson's Creek near Springfield, Missouri, one of the Confederate regiments was the South Kansas-Texas regiment, suggestung that some pro-Confederate Kansans had enlisted for the Southern cause after escaping to secessionist Texas.

Not all Kansans were at home when the first shots of the war were fired. Many were in Washington, D.C., seeking appointments to government jobs in the newest state. The day after the first guns opened on Fort Sumter, James H. Lane, a new senator from Kansas, climbed up on a dry goods box in Washington to make a speech. It was his first night in the nation's capital at Willard's Hotel. An excited crowd filled Pennsylvania Avenue on that night when Fort Sumter surrendered. When Lane stepped up, cries from Southern sympathizers in the crowd called for him to be mobbed and hanged.

"Mob, and be damned!" he shouted, his eyes flashing.

> Mob, and be damned! I have a hundred men from Kansas in this crowd, all armed; all fighting men; just from the victims fields of Kansas! They will shoot every damned man of you who again cries, "Mob. Mob."

The loyal members of the crowd cheered, and Lane speechified uninterrupted.

He was as good as his word, too. Only three days after Fort Sumter surrendered, shortly before 9 P.M. on April 18, 1861, Senator Lane and about fifty Kansans arrived at the White House, where they were given arms and ammunition. Lane received a sword that he prized throughout the war. These men were mustered in as the Frontier Guards, organized with Lane as captain. When rumors flew that the nation's capital might be attacked, Lane advised the War Department that the Frontier Guards were available.

Shortly afterward, a mob of Southern sympathizers in Baltimore attacked the Sixth Massachusetts Infantry Regiment in that city some thirty miles from Washington, and the War

Department received a message that President Lincoln was about to be kidnapped. Lane was ordered to muster his men to protect the president. For the next eight days, the Frontier Guards served on guard duty around the Executive Mansion in daylight hours; at night they bivouacked in the East Room of the White House. Once, while serving in the presidential home, a detachment of the Kansans ventured across the Potomac River to capture a Rebel flag in Virginia.

J.B. Stockton, the second lieutenant of the Frontier Guards, boasted that he "captured the first rebel flag of the rebellion . . . at or near Falls Church, Virginia." He and some of his men were testing secessionist strength, and upon seeing a company of Virginia militia drilling, the Kansans charged. The Rebels fled without their flag, so Stockton took it down and delivered

*Lane's jayhawkers made secessionists pay
a high price for their disloyalty.*

it to Jim Lane. Senator Lane hung it on the balcony outside his window at Washington's Willard Hotel with his scrawled hand-writing proclaiming *"Captured by the Frontier Guards upon the sacred soil of Virginia!"*

Washington was not immediately attacked, however, and on April 25, Jim Lane's Frontier Guards were thanked personally and officially disbanded by President Lincoln himself.

At home in Kansas, patriotic fervor swept the border with Missouri, from White Cloud in the extreme northeastern cor-ner where the Missouri River snips off a part of the state's rec-tangle south to Leavenworth, all the way south to Fort Scott. Companies of men were recruited, and officers for them were elected. Members of many of the companies were all from the same town, community, or county; their officers were typically well-known and influential men in the community.

When the officers reported their companies ready for duty, they were organized into regiments. Most of them were anx-ious to see action because most people on both sides assumed the war would be short-lived. Old rivalries and grudges were dredged up against the border ruffians in Missouri, many of whom were now secessionists.

Not all communities in the young state were sure they wanted to contribute recruits to the president's call for volun-teers. At a meeting in the former proslave town of Atchison on April 17, 1861, the formation of a company to help subdue the rebellion was voted down. Many Atchison men felt "coercion" was not the way to deal with the South. Several even echoed the sentiments of secessionist Gov. Claiborne F. Jackson of Missouri who replied to Lincoln's call by stating on the same day, "Not one man will the State of Missouri furnish to carry on such an unholy crusade."

In May 1861, the 1st Kansas Volunteer Infantry Regiment was formed at Leavenworth. The Frontier Guards were not the only ones who could capture secesh banners. On June 3, 1861, a Rebel flag was seized at Iatan, Missouri. It was brought to Leavenworth by a dozen Kansans, enlistees in a company calling themselves the Elwood Guards and another, the Leavenworth Steuben Guards, a company of German immigrants.

Both companies became part of the new 1st Kansas Volunteer Infantry Regiment. The capture of the Rebel flag created intense excitement. Many prominent people in Leavenworth, the largest city in the state at the time, opposed the act on the grounds it was illegal, while the Leavenworth *Daily Conservative* editorially supported it.

Ten days later, seven companies—including those that had captured the Iatan flag—departed from Leavenworth for service in nearby Kansas City and northwest Missouri, a secessionist stronghold and one that produced many border ruffians during the "bleeding Kansas" era. But the matter of the Rebel pennant was not ended. In the weekly *Leavenworth Herald,* R. C. Satterlee charged Daniel R. Anthony, owner and editor of the *Conservative,* with lying about the Iatan flag affair.

The charge led to a shooting fray in the streets of Leavenworth in which Satterlee was killed. Anthony, the ardent abolitionist with a volatile temper, was tried before a Unionist judge in Leavenworth and promptly acquitted. Anthony went on to become lieutenant colonel of the notorious 7th Kansas—"Jennison's Jayhawkers"—and was appointed provost marshal of Kansas City by Jim Lane when he returned from Washington, D.C.

Other regiments from Kansas were organized in 1861 and the earliest volunteers enlisted for ninety days. They were equipped and uniformed from existing and available resources warehoused at Fort Riley, Fort Leavenworth, and Fort Scott, the three military installations in Kansas. The uniforms provided at the beginning of the war were adequate to clothe a Kansas soldier for a year.

When their clothing allowance was spent, replacement articles were paid for from their meager wages of thirteen dollars per month. In some cases, the Kansas soldiers wore items sent from home and, as was the case with many Jayhawkers, they wore clothing taken wherever they found it.

Early in the war, prices for replacement uniform items included: hats, $1.80; jackets, $6.25; trousers, $4.15; overcoats, $10.55; blankets, $3.60; boots, $3.25 a pair; plumes for cavalry hats, fifteen cents; hat cords and tassels, fifteen cents; hat edge and crossed swords insignia, two cents; and forage caps, sixty-five cents.

If the Kansas regiments went to war often dressed in a hodgepodge, their armaments were equally mixed. They were armed company by company with whatever type of weapon was available. Some companies carried converted flintlock muskets or crudely rifled smoothbores. Others were issued foreign-made weapons. More than a few chose instead to acquire rifles of their own preference at their own expense or to carry their own personal firearms from home.

Discipline in most of the Kansas regiments started out loose and degenerated rapidly. Leaders of the Free-State territorial struggle frequently were elected as ideal candidates for officers in a war most Kansans viewed as a conflict to end slavery. One was led by James Montgomery, the small, dark-haired funda-mentalist preacher and abolitionist who had come to Kansas in the midst of the troubled territorial days and taken up resi-dence near Fort Scott.

Founded along the Marmaton River in what became south-eastern Kansas in the 1840s as a dragoon post for the protec-tion of the Santa Fe Trail, Fort Scott had been abandoned by the U.S. Army in the 1850s. By the first year of the war, it would become a major Union depot in the Trans-Mississippi West during the Civil War. In Montgomery's time, the empty fron-tier post had provided its buildings as the nucleus of a com-munity of proslavery settlers.

Most were Missourians from the more populated area east across the state line. Some were driven from homesteads fur-ther north in Kansas by Free Staters and had settled anew in the less populated part of the state. Montgomery brought his views and assertive personality to bear against the slave interests.

Jennison was a new leader who showed up after

Charles R. Jennison.

Montgomery, a flashy, even outlandishly dressed dude who nonetheless appealed to Free-State Kansans and who was trusted by Montgomery. These two leaders had become adept at organizing vigilante companies in southeast Kansas during the territorial era, and in early 1861 they were instrumental in organizing the 3rd, 4th, 5th, and 7th Kansas Volunteer regiments.

Montgomery was elected colonel of the 3rd, while Jennison made sure he was voted in as colonel of the 7th since he had recruited the regiment. Not all these recruits were Kansans, either. An entire company of the 7th Kansas was from Ohio, in the vicinity where once had lived old John Brown, who had perpetrated the massacre of proslavery men and been active in the Underground Railroad in Kansas till his disastrous raid on Harper's Ferry in 1859. The company's captain was even one of Old Brown's numerous sons.

These men frequently saw the war as an opportunity for vengeance and punishment of the Missouri border ruffians for their flagrant intrusions before statehood. Their attitudes carried forward to the men they commanded, permitting looting, pillaging, torchings, and even murder. Only a minimum of restraint was applied, and little military discipline was exerted during the first year of the war.

Sen. Jim Lane believed he saw an opportunity to seize military as well as political power—after Gov. Charles Robinson had recruited the 1st and 2nd Kansas Volunteers for Federal service—so he tendered to President Lincoln two additional regiments for three years or the duration of the war, whichever came first.

Lincoln assumed that Lane was not only a political friend but also serious about creating regiments for Federal service. The president had his secretary of war commission Lane as a brigadier general of volunteers, with authority to raise troops, a privilege usually reserved for a state's governor.

Although Lane had to give up his commission in order to keep his senatorial seat, he and others like Montgomery and Jennison still busily organized not two but three volunteer

"Fort Union," Lane's headquarters near Kansas City.

regiments. The 3rd Kansas Volunteers, commanded by Montgomery, the 4th Kansas Volunteers, under William Weer, and the 5th Kansas with Hamilton P. Johnson at its head were known as the "Kansas Brigade," or "Lane's Brigade." Lane was intent upon pillaging the Missouri border, burning farms and homes to the ground, freeing slaves, and ferreting out anyone his men considered disloyal. Kansans had seen their share of fighting during the territorial era, but they were anxious to see action again.

On May 20, 1861, Capt. Nathaniel Lyon of Fort Riley was promoted to brigadier general, and shortly afterward he led troops in pursuit of the pro-Southern Missouri governor. His troops were outnumbered by the Confederates of Gen. Sterling Price. Nevertheless, Lyon led his small army, including the 1st and 2nd Kansas Volunteers, into battle at Wilson's Creek, some dozen miles from Springfield, Missouri, on August 10. There the Kansans got all the fight they wanted.

The Federal government's 1861 policy to maintain control of Missouri left General Lyon with no choice but to stand or abandon the state to the Confederacy. A whirlwind summer campaign brought him and his small army to southwestern Missouri at the end of July. He advanced his forces south toward Springfield. Lyon discovered that the Missouri army he pursued had joined forces with another army of Louisianians, some Texans, and a brigade of Arkansas volunteers, and now clearly outnumbered the Union troops.

Confronted by the larger Southern army, the feisty Union general reluctantly ordered an about-face and headed back on the road to Springfield, the largest town in the area. The Confederates, under the combined command of Sterling Price and Gen. Benjamin McCulloch, tried to flank Lyon's tired infantrymen and cut off his retreat but only succeeded in catching up. Lyon's rearguard, including elements of the Kansas regiments, fought a delaying skirmish at Dug Springs on August 2, 1861. The infantrymen held their ground against Rebel cavalrymen.

A troop of United States cavalry regulars returned from the main Union column to charge into a brigade of advancing Missourians and scattered the whole of Price's part of the Southern army like a youngster throwing a rock against the side of a chicken coop. The Kansans jeered and made rude jokes about the fleeing "huckleberries" after only about 50 Yanks dispersed 1,500 Rebels. After the sharp skirmish with Rebels at Dug Springs on that hot August day, the 2nd Kansas led the advance from Springfield to the east.

On August 6, eight companies of the 1st Kansas and part of the 2nd Kansas turned out when a Union patrol clashed with a party of Sterling Price's cavalry. Thinking the Missourians were about to attack, the Kansans remained on the alert well into the night. After dispatching a message to St. Louis seeking reinforcements on August 9, Lyon learned that some Union regulars and Company I, 2nd Kansas Volunteers had fought another of Price's mounted patrols at Grand Prairie, about five miles west of Springfield.

These actions, combined with the eminent enlistment expirations among many of the units in his army, convinced Lyon to attack the next day. The entire army left Springfield for Grand Prairie, and as they marched the Kansans sang "The Happy Land of Canaan." At about 5 A.M., Col. George W. Deitzler of the 1st Kansas received orders to launch the attack that opened the Battle of Wilson's Creek. As he led his Kansans into position, Deitzler rode along his regiment's line and exclaimed, "Boys, we've got them, damn them!"

The regiment then drove the Confederates from Bloody Hill for the first time that day, then continued to advance until stopped by shelling by the Rebel Pulaski Arkansas Battery. Nothing could hold the Southern ranks against the determined Kansans. The Rebels broke ranks and abandoned the hill.

The battle raged back and forth until 9 A.M., when Price launched a horrific attack along Lyon's entire front. The Union soldiers were alerted to the attack. Pockets of desperately fighting men of both sides developed among the hills and hollows, on the prairie, and in the woods. Federals and Confederates alike found themselves engulfed by a blanket of smoke that choked and blinded. Eyes tearing, throats clogging, they fought doggedly on that morning. The 1st Kansas was hard pressed, and Lyon received his first wound while rallying them.

When it looked as if the Union lines were about to give way, Lyon ordered the 1st Iowa and the 2nd Kansas into the battle, and the 1st Kansas retired to regroup.

As he led the 2nd Kansas to the front, Lyon received his second and fatal wound at about 9:30 A.M. The Iowa and Kansas troops viciously drove Price's Missourians onto the defensive. Swinging his hat, Lyon called out to the Kansans, "Come on, my bully boys, I will lead you; forward!" But then the head of the attack, in column by platoons, was ambushed on the slope of Bloody Hill. Confederate riflemen launched a hail of fire into the 2nd Kansas.

Volley after volley showered into the men following Lyon and the extraordinary leader, Col. Robert B. Mitchell. A rush of the Kansans and Iowans, among the latter future Kansas poet laureate Sgt. Eugene F. Ware, surged up Bloody Hill trying to reach the Rebel infantry, but the Southerners simply lowered their fire and raked the Union troops until the attack became disorganized and threatened to break apart. Among those cut down were General Lyon and Col. Robert B. Mitchell of the 2nd Kansas. Lyon was the first general to be killed in the Civil War. Lt. Gustavus Schreyer and two men of his company of the 2nd Kansas carried Lyon's body to the rear. Mitchell was so badly wounded that he was carried from the field.

The ferocious volley of musketry that struck down Lyon and Mitchell caused Company K, the leading unit of the 2nd Kansas, to stagger. Yet as the Missourians reloaded for another volley the Kansans pressed forward. After a quarter hour of desperate combat, they drove the secessionists from the hill.

Lt. Col. Charles Blair reformed his regiment at the crest of Bloody Hill. There they dodged falling branches as artillery intended for their ranks overshot their marks. Lieutenant

Colonel Blair assumed command of the 2nd Kansas and hastened to the field hospital where Mitchell lay. The colonel told Blair that he "must take command, and fight the regiment to the best of his ability." Blair replied, "I will try not to disgrace you or the State."

Five hours into the battle, both Kansas regiments had been ravaged. The 2nd Kansas and several companies of the 1st Kansas anchored the Federal right. About 10 A.M., Southern troops from Arkansas and Louisiana counterattacked. Blair lost a horse to rifle fire, and his men had nearly exhausted their ammunition. When Blair received the order to retire, he said he "was humiliated beyond expression for . . . [he] felt that the battle might have been ours."

Nevertheless, his Kansans left the hill "in good order and slow time, with the men perfectly dressed as on the drill ground." The Battle of Wilson's Creek, where the mettle of Kansas soldiers was first tested, ended in a Rebel victory but proved Kansans made outstanding soldiers.

In the meantime, Jim Lane's men were also acquiring a reputation, but not the same as those in Lyon's army. The senator with a general's rank recruited his brigade along the Missouri border. Many of the men who enlisted remembered Lane as the fire-eating Free-State leader ready to meet the border ruffians blow for blow. They enlisted at Lane's call and promised to make the secessionists pay a high price for their disloyalty. As the 1st and 2nd Kansas regiments were licking their wounds from Wilson's Creek, the 3rd, 4th, and 5th Kansas regiments prepared to teach Missourians a lesson.

Lane's unruly, undertrained, and undisciplined men scattered into the Missouri counties east of Fort Scott, prompting General Price to send Brig. Gen. James S. Rains—who was also a Missouri senator and much more comfortable behind a desk than on a horse at the head of a regiment—with a force of cavalry "to clear them out." When Rains reported that Lane's men were too numerous for him to take on alone, Price, fresh from the victory at Wilson's Creek, marched to his support.

On September 2, 1861, a small advance guard of Confederates stumbled upon a company of Lane's Brigade at Drywood Creek. They skirmished for an hour or so before the Kansans hightailed it away with the Missourians in hot pursuit till nightfall. While Price wrote off the engagement as a "trifle," Lane claimed he had repulsed Rains but was forced to fall back because of Price's superior numbers. Casualties were light, with only a few Kansans killed or wounded, but Colonel Weer lost the mules that provided transportation for his 4th Kansas regiment.

Jennison's incomplete 7th Kansas had been left behind at Fort Scott. They pillaged the town that had grown up in and around the buildings of the old frontier post, even though most of the citizens other than a couple of women had departed. Price felt he had chastised Lane sufficiently and marched for Lexington on the Missouri River. Lane sent Colonel Johnson's 5th Kansas and Jennison's 7th Kansas regiments in a rather lackluster pursuit. They followed the Confederates for a while, then returned with some 200 head of cattle and a number of freed slaves called "contrabands."

On September 22, 1861, Lane advanced his brigade to Osceola, a town he promptly burned to the ground. Osceola was at the head of navigation on the Osage River and had a population of a couple of thousand. It was a commercial center that some inclined to jealousy reported as a major secessionist supply depot. Whether it was or was not, Jim Lane ordered advance scouts to investigate. They returned and complained that the townspeople had fired on them.

Lane ordered fellow Jayhawker James Montgomery and the 3rd Kansas Volunteer Regiment to follow the mounted advance guard into the town to show them what happened when they shot at Kansans in Union uniforms. The horsemen rumbled down the main street firing their handguns indiscriminately. Montgomery's men secured the town, arresting those who resisted. Lane arrived not long afterward.

An inspection of the town revealed warehouses full of lead,

powder, cartridge papers, and camp equipment. Perhaps this was a Rebel depot, but more common supplies such as sacks of flour, sugar, and molasses, coffee, bacon, and other things that might be found in any town were also confiscated. Indeed, they found so much to confiscate that they impressed stolen horses and wagons and carriages, one of which soon showed up at Lane's home in Lawrence.

While the Jayhawkers were loading the wagons, Lane supervised a drumhead court-martial and shooting of about nine private citizens and announced that Osceola had to be "knocked into Herculaneum." The courthouse and all but three of the houses, whose owners could prove their loyalty beyond a shadow of a doubt, were burned to ashes. Along with the wagonloads of booty, the Kansans' plunder included hundreds of horses, mules, cattle, and freed slaves.

From Osceola, Lane made a left turn and marched north toward Kansas City, leaving in the wake of his brigade such destruction that Sherman might have taken lessons for his later March to the Sea. Lane told his men, "Everything disloyal, from a Shanghai rooster to a Durham cow, must be cleared out." The Lane Brigade's depredations was reckoned to be in the millions of dollars, and Lane's personal reputation forged ahead of him.

Slaves by the dozens left their owners and joined him all along the road. They sometimes brought with them livestock, horses, good wagons, and even an occasional carriage. When mildly reprimanded for the looting, Lane replied that more Jayhawkers should be enlisted as the quickest way to stamp out treason. During the campaigning in the fall of 1861, the Lane Brigade and the 7th Kansas Volunteer Cavalry became the hated scourge of the frontier. Their tactics also caused many Missourians who might otherwise have remained ambivalent to side with the irregulars.

In response to the vicious attack on Osceola, which Kansans dubbed a battle while Missourians called an outrage, the autumn of 1861 brought retaliatory raids by Missourians to a number of communities in eastern Kansas. These towns suffered in part for the actions of the Kansas units in Federal service. Both Humboldt, an Allen County community that had just been attacked a month earlier, and Gardner, a Johnson County town, were raided by Missouri bushwhackers in October 1861.

A report from Humboldt stated that the Southerners

> after taking whatever they could make available in the way of dry goods and groceries . . . announced their intention of burning the town. The hellish work commenced, and before they desisted 21 dwelling houses, stores and a mill were consumed—more than one-half the buildings.

This variety of guerrilla warfare was conducted throughout much of the war, and the tone was set by the Lane Brigade. The Confederates have often been blamed for the violent nature of this war, but the difference was that the Kansans had the advantage and legitimacy of being inducted into Federal service while the Missourians often rode in gangs or, at best, loosely organized militia. The Missourians also perfected guerrilla tactics. At various times Kansas troops raided widely in the western part of Missouri.

The 7th Kansas became so notorious for raiding that the regiment became known as "Jennison's Jayhawkers" after its first colonel, Charles R. Jennison. Both the 7th Kansas and the Lane Brigade freed slaves, stole livestock, stocked Kansas stores with contraband goods, and plundered homes and businesses. Sometimes their victims were Missourians who were not sympathetic to the Confederacy or even loyal and strong Unionists.

Kansas City was a fledgling center of business on the Missouri River in 1861. It witnessed an exodus of its mercantile houses as the Kansas soldiers entered, only to be followed by vengeance-seeking Rebel guerrillas. Nearly all the major businesses moved to Leavenworth to avoid trouble with the bushwhackers. Kansas City's *Journal of Commerce*, a weekly business newspaper, suspended publication in August 1861.

The U.S. Army in 1860 had moved its supply depot from Fort Leavenworth to Kansas City to improve the supplying of military forts along the Santa Fe Trail, the Oregon Trail, and in Kansas, New Mexico, and Indian Territory. Now the supply depot and the commercial houses as well moved to Leavenworth to reside under the umbrella of protection provided by the fort. Even Kansas City's two banks were not immune. About $80,000 in gold was carried under the guard of two companies of soldiers to a ferry boat and then were transported to the fort. Later the cash was shipped down the Missouri River by steamboat to be deposited in parent banks in St. Louis.

As Kansas City was threatened by the Lane Brigade from the south, it was beleaguered by "Jennison's Jayhawkers" from the north. Jennison and the officers and men of the 7th Kansas were from some very unsavory elements around Leavenworth, and some of the regiment practiced up by sacking the saloons of that Kansas town before crossing into Missouri in November. They went there theoretically to protect Union supply trains and warehouses in Jackson County, put down "rebels," and "loyalize" the residents in the vicinity.

Most Kansans tended to consider all Missourians as "rebels," so they rationalized the depredations of Jennison's outfit just as they did Lane's brigade. Only one serious skirmish with Confederates under "Colonel" Upton Hayes marked the campaign of the 7th in Missouri. The rest of 1861 and early 1862 saw the regiment assuring that Missouri "citizens were given a little touch of the misfortunes of war," as Daniel R. Anthony wrote.

As one private soldier in the 7th Kansas observed, "Every house along our line of march but one was burned, and off on our left flank for miles, columns of smoke from burning houses and barns could be seen."

Kansans at home generally approved of the actions of Lane, Jim Montgomery, Jennison, Anthony, and their thugs. This was partly due to a growing anti-slavery fervor that applauded the slave-stealing activities and partly because old animosities still rankled. But another big reason was because men like Anthony controlled the media—Anthony himself owned the Leavenworth *Daily Conservative,* the single most influential newspaper in Kansas during the war. These editors glamorized that exploits of the Jayhawkers while falsely portraying all of Missouri in rebellion.

As Kansans convinced themselves of the justice of jayhawking, Missourians grew a bitter, impassioned hatred toward Kansans. Upton Hayes, who put up the only fight against the 7th Kansas, had been a freighter in the Santa Fe trade before the war. He initially tried to remain neutral but took up arms for the South after Jayhawkers burned one of his wagon trains and his home and stole his cattle, oxen, horses, and slaves. Hayes had little difficulty recruiting other guerrillas for his irregular unit.

Neither did other pro-Southern leaders, men such as "Colonel Talbot," who raided Humboldt, or "Sheriff Clem," who raided and killed three men in Linn County, Kansas, or an especially cruel leader named William Clarke Quantrill who made a brutal raid on Aubrey in Johnson County, Kansas. Quantrill and his men shot down unarmed civilians in cold blood. All along the Kansas-Missouri border, attacks brought retaliation, which brought counter-retaliation, increasing by 1862 into widespread violence and brutality.

The Missouri border was not the only one that Kansas needed to be concerned about. Trouble also brewed in the western part of the state and on its southern border. Before statehood, Kansas Territory stretched west to the summit of the Rocky Mountains. The area included the foothills of the Rockies— indeed, the town of Denver was named after a territorial governor of Kansas. When a state constitution was written, legislators declined to include both agricultural laws and mining laws because of the recent discovery of gold in Cherry Creek and the subsequent rush to the gold fields near Denver. So when Kansas became a state, the western boundary was set along the 100th meridian, lopping off the mountains and some of the high plains and delegating them to the new Colorado Territory.

Denver grew rapidly until the war commenced. The city was served by three routes or trails—the northern route along the Platte River to Julesburg, Colorado Territory; the southern route along the Santa Fe Trail past Big Timbers on the Arkansas River to Bent's Fort, then north along the east slope; and the central route from various points on the Missouri River along the Kansas and Smoky Hill rivers straight to Denver. The gold rush attracted plenty of legitimate miners but also some unsavory characters, and they came from both North and South. Early in 1861, Denver witnessed a series of confrontations between Southern sympathizers and Union men. Chief among the pro-Confederates was Charley Harrison, a native of Arkansas and a known shootist.

Harrison stood at medium height with a slender build, rapidly balding but with a luxuriant beard. He was described by a contemporary as "suave, gracious, quietly forceful if the occasion arose, and always attired in black broadcloth, the personification of a Southern gentleman in appearance and public behavior." Rarely one to start a fight, he never backed down from one. He wore two Colts revolvers on his belt and knew how to use them.

Southerners represented about a third of Denver's population, and they collected around Harrison, who held court in the Criterion Saloon. On April 24, 1861, Denver citizens awoke to find the Stars and Bars floating over the building next to the saloon. It wasn't long before Union and Southern sympathizers had squared off, and the Northern leader—a bear of a man named Sam Logan—stood coat button-to-coat button with Harrison. Cooler heads prevailed.

Harrison's cohorts became known as "Bummers." Many of the Unionists enlisted in the 1st Colorado Volunteer Infantry Regiment. The Bummers and Company B of the 1st Colorado brawled, once even inside the Criterion Saloon. The Bummers finally were driven underground by weight of numbers.

But when the Union supporters won out, some of the Southerners began to plot to disrupt communication and trade along the Santa Fe Trail. About two thirds of that trail stretched across Kansas. It not only served as a supply route to keep food and fodder flowing out to the forts in New Mexico and Arizona but also was the southern link with resources in California. Cutting this slender lifeline could give the Confederacy vital control of the crucial American West.

The increased traffic on the Santa Fe Trail caused yet another military problem for the young state. Southern Plains Indians resented the almost constant incursions into their country, and tensions ran high on the high plains during 1861 and 1862. Some of the military units were heading west to fight Rebels, and early in 1862 New Mexico Territory was saved from Confederate invasion by a fight at Valverde. Other bluecoats, however, marched down the Santa Fe Trail to quell uprisings of Apache and Navajo further west. With battle against Indians in the offing, it was a simple matter to treat all Indians with disdain, even to mistreat those on the trail along the way. Animosities would lead to an Indian war on the Kansas plains before the war between the whites had been resolved.

But the wild Indians on the plains were not the only red men to threaten a Kansas border. In late 1861 still another threat arose. In October, skirmishes occurred between Confederate and Union factions of the Creek tribe. The Creeks were one of the so-called Five Civilized Tribes, tribes of Native Americans who had been removed from the southeastern United States in the 1830s and 1840s. Besides the Creeks, there were Cherokee, Choctaw, Chickasaw, and Seminole. Most of these tribes were split between the two warring sides of white men.

When Col. Douglas Cooper, once a trusted agent to the Choctaw but now a Confederate officer, arrived in the Creek Nation of Indian Territory, he found between 3,500 and as many as 6,000 pro-Union Creek, some Seminole, and a few African-Americans who had escaped slavery and fled to the

Many Creek, Seminole, and Cherokee suffered and died from severe cold, exposure, and starvation.

Nations. These people gathered near the home of Creek Chief Opothleyoholo, and small bands of his pro-Union warriors clashed with patrols of pro-Confederate Creek leaders Daniel and Chilly McIntosh.

Cooper sought a meeting with Opothleyoholo, but the old chief refused not only to meet but even to reply to Cooper's written request. Opothleyoholo had been in contact with a U.S. Indian agent in Kansas who encouraged him to resist the Confederate overtures and promised that Federal troops would soon cross the border into Indian Territory and help the loyal Indians drive the Rebels out. Cooper determined to mount a campaign "and either compel submission" to the Confederacy or "drive him and his party from the country."

By November 15, 1861, Colonel Cooper had pulled together about 900 Indian soldiers from the 1st Choctaw and Chickasaw Mounted Rifles, the 1st Seminole Cavalry Battalion, the 1st Creek Cavalry, and some 500 volunteers of the 9th Texas Cavalry who had been assigned to support the Confederate Indians. The Indian soldiers wore no uniforms but rather civilian clothing of wool or cotton with trade blankets. They carried a variety of weapons from shotguns to hunting rifles, and from knives to tomahawks. They were dressed and armed almost identically with their pro-Union counterparts.

Opothleyoholo prudently moved his multitude to more plentiful grazing for the large amount of livestock and to be nearer the Kansas border from which he had been assured succor would come. Unencumbered by women, children, the aged, and all of their baggage, Cooper's force caught up with the fleeing Creeks.

The Texans with Cooper pursued a band of Union Creeks at about 4 P.M. on November 19, only to learn they were really decoys. As dusk settled, the Creek scouts led the Texans to a line of timber along a stream at a place known as Round Mound. The wily old Opothleyoholo sprang his trap, but when the Confederate Indians joined the fray the Union Creeks fired the prairie to cover their retreat from the Battle of Round Mound.

The pursuit continued for ten days until Cooper attempted to envelope the retreating Creeks between two columns. But confusion ensued and at Opothleyoholo's camp on Bird Creek most of the 1st Cherokee Mounted Rifles deserted because of their opposition to the unjust and relentless pursuit of the Union Creeks. By the time the Confederates recovered from the disaster early in December, Opothleyoholo planned another fight on his own terms along Bird Creek on December 9, 1861.

Fearing that the victories at Round Mountain and Bird Creek and the desertion of the 1st Cherokee would shift the loyalty of Indian Territory to the Union, Cooper called to Arkansas for help. A column of 1,600 Texas and Arkansas cavalry who did not fall for any of the Creek tricks punished the Union Indians severely at the Battle of Patriot Hills. In a running fight, many Creek warriors were killed or wounded, women and children were captured, and livestock and supplies seized as booty. Gathering together the survivors of his group, Opothleyoholo set out immediately for Kansas.

Throughout the winter the Creeks and Seminoles attempted to survive in several crowded camps in southeastern Kansas. They were joined by Union Cherokees who had mutinied from the 1st Cherokee and their families. Literally thousands of these Indians had fled to the relative safety of Kansas. Many suffered and died from severe cold, exposure, and starvation in camps from near Eureka in Greenwood County to Yates Center in Woodson County and Lebo in Coffey County.

The first nine months after the firing on Fort Sumter had brought about some occurrences on the frontier that would later help define the war in Kansas. Early in the national conflict, militia companies were formed, usually in geographical units but also containing the core of old Free-State militia outfits from the "bleeding Kansas" days. These companies were organized into regiments, and some of them saw action in conventional battle at Wilson's Creek while others took vengeance against Missouri for the acts of border ruffians during the territorial era.

Jayhawking became an art in the first year of the war. Concern about Indians in the western part of the state and south of the Kansas border also posed a threat that needed to be addressed. During 1862, Kansans would feel the reaction to jayhawking by Missouri bushwhackers, help secure Missouri for the Union, and organize unique regiments in the Federal service.

CHAPTER 2

"Overrun with Thieves and Highway Robbers": 1862

In 1862 there was serious fighting west of the Mississippi River. The reorganized 1st Kansas and the more disciplined 7th Kansas regiments saw action in the Confederate state of Mississippi. Union Maj. Gen. William S. Rosecrans operated against the Rebels at Corinth and the two Kansas regiments were part of his Yankee army.

In addition to Corinth, the 7th also saw action in battles at Rienzi, Iuka, and Buzzard Roost Station. It was ultimately ordered to Tennessee, where it was added to Ulysses S. Grant's campaign against Vicksburg. The 8th Kansas went to Corinth, joined by the 2nd Kansas Battery en route. Both saw some action in Mississippi and Alabama before the artillery unit got orders to head north to join Union Gen. Don Carlos Buell to defend Louisville and Cincinnati.

The year 1862 opened with more jayhawking on New Year's Day when Lt. Col. Daniel R. Anthony led 200 7th Kansas Cavalry and a 12-pounder into Dayton, Missouri, at dawn. All but one of the forty-six homes in the hamlet were destroyed.

A week after the raid on Dayton, Anthony led part of the 7th Kansas into Pleasant Hill on another jayhawking raid. One of the victimized townspeople wrote: "Anthony . . . took away ten thousand dollars worth of stock & 55 negroes. This is the third time the Kansas troops have been in our town &

carried away not less than 150 thousand dollars worth of property."

Moving on and bivouacking near the partially destroyed village of Morristown, Anthony's Jayhawkers completed its destruction. A soldier in the 7th Kansas wrote to a newspaper back home: "There are only five houses standing now. . . . I think when we leave it, it will be known only by name. . . . am inclined to think that the secesh suffered *some* while we were among them, for you could see smoke in all directions."

Under orders from the top commander of all Federal armies Gen. Henry Halleck, Gen. John Pope launched a campaign in mid-January to drive Jim Lane's brigade and Jennison's 7th Kansas Cavalry under Anthony back to Kansas. General Halleck described the Kansas troops:

> They are no better than a band of robbers; they cross the line, rob, steal, plunder, and burn whatever they can lay hands upon. They disgrace the name and uniform of American soldiers and are driving good Union men into the ranks of the secession army.

By early February, Pope had been called back east to command the Army of the Potomac at the Second Battle of Bull Run. Gen. David Hunter, who replaced him, placed all of Kansas under martial law in an attempt to control the Jayhawkers. Eventually, Hunter stationed troops in northeast Kansas when Judge Samuel Kingman of the state supreme court declared that Kansans were as fearful of Jayhawkers as they were of Rebels from Missouri.

Missouri artist and political observer George Caleb Bingham opined in a letter to a Missouri legislator that Jennison should be hanged for "if he were hung [Confederate Gen. Sterling] Price would lose thereby the best recruiting officer he has ever had." Bingham said that previously Jennison "had been murdering and stealing 'on his own hook,'" but now he was a U.S. Army colonel with a regiment of cavalry "with a view . . . to test upon more extensive scale, the efficacy of indiscriminate pillage and rapine in crushing out rebellion."

Bingham provided an example on February 12 when he wrote of the plight of Henry Younger, a pro-Union stockman and farmer on the Missouri side of the state line; he had lost $4,000 worth of wagons and carriages plus forty saddle horses to 7th Kansas Jayhawkers. The treatment of their family eventually caused Younger's sons Cole and Jim to be heard from later in 1862 as Rebel guerrillas.

On March 22, 1862, Yankee cavalry under Kansan Maj. James Pomeroy surrounded a farm house, ordering the occupants to surrender. The Rebels fired on Pomeroy's company, wounding the major, and then escaped. The attack was intended to end the career of William Clarke Quantrill. The bushwhacker leader had made a murderous raid on Aubry, so Federal authorities determined to crush him before his virulent strain of guerrilla warfare spread.

In retaliation for raids by Lane's Brigade and Jennison's Jayhawkers in the 7th Kansas Cavalry, guerrillas with Quantrill looted the town of all they could carry, burned a house, and fled through Federal lines back into Missouri.

Among the Unionists in Aubry was Abraham Ellis, formerly a superintendent of schools in Miami County, Kansas, near Paola. Before the war, one of his school masters had been none other than William Clarke Quantrill. Ellis spent the night in Aubry's hotel after appealing for protection of the border from Southern vigilantes. When Ellis looked out of his window to see what all the commotion was about, Quantrill himself shot his former employer in the forehead.

"In a few minutes," Ellis recalled, "Quantrill came . . . & then recognized me & got a cloth and some water & washed my face & said he did it himself & was damned sorry for it—as I was one of the Kansas men he did *not* want to hurt." Ellis became known as "Bullet Hole" Ellis because he survived but was forever marked by the hole the ball left in his forehead.

Although Quantrill, the guerrilla leader, and part of his band were in the house, surrounded by Pomeroy's detachment, they made their getaway to strike again in the future. He was soon captured by a posse and locked in a Paola jail. But because the posse was not a military unit but rather under civil law, Southern sympathizers secured Quantrill's release on a writ of *habeas corpus* and he slipped safely across the border into Missouri. The guerrilla war spiraled between attack and retaliation through the rest of 1862.

During the early months of 1862, the Creeks, Seminoles, and Cherokees who had fled to Kansas suffered severely from the cold, harsh winter weather. Many froze to death, and when disease broke out from unsanitary conditions, more died of sickness. As early as January 15, Opothleyoholo described conditions to General Hunter.

It was a newspaperman, however—Daniel Webster Wilder, editor of Anthony's Leavenworth *Daily Conservative*—who remarked on this potential source of manpower for the Union. He observed "between six and seven thousand Indians, refugees from the Rebels. . . . Among these Indians . . . are about 2,000 warriors . . . who only need arms and ammunition to make them a useful force."

By the end of 1862, three regiments of home guards were organized from among the Indians and became the Kansas Indian Brigade.

Early in 1862, some of the volunteers who enlisted in Kansas regiments bore terrible witness to the less than glorious side of soldiering during the Civil War. According to the state adjutant general's report, Richard S. Peters, private, Company K, 9th Kansas Cavalry, died of measles. Peters had enlisted in October 1861, and was mustered in on January 16, 1862, with the rest of his company. He became one of the victims of a measles epidemic that swept through the 9th Kansas for a month, finally running its course in March 1862.

Another soldier, Pvt. William K. Nickel, D Company, 6th Kansas Cavalry, enlisted on September 14, 1862, and was mustered in the same day along with thirty-five other members of his company from Trading Post in Linn County, Kansas. He succumbed to illness at Neosho, Missouri, across the border from Fort Scott only five months later, along with six other men of his company. Another half-dozen were discharged for disabilities brought about by disease within the next six months.

Joseph K. Smith, too, was mustered into the 6th Kansas Cavalry as assistant surgeon, more or less the equivalent of modern medical corpsmen. Smith's career as an assistant surgeon was cut short less than six months after his enlistment when, ironically, he died of disease at Fort Scott on August 2, 1862. During the war, more Kansans died of disease than the regiment lost in killed, wounded, and captured troops.

On April 1, 1862, Robert B. Mitchell and James G. Blunt were promoted to brigadier general. Mitchell was hero of Wilson's Creek, a taciturn man who commanded respect and would be a competent commander east of the Mississippi. Blunt was the short, thickly built, black-haired and black-eyed lieutenant colonel of the 3rd Kansas, commanded by Col. James Montgomery, and himself an abolitionist and favored by Montgomery and Lane.

Mitchell would serve in Kentucky and Tennessee in 1862. Blunt would make a name for himself as a successful commander by the end of the year. Blunt's appointment was influenced by Sen. James H. Lane and was obviously political. Nevertheless, both of these generals from Kansas were among the few with military training and experience. They performed well militarily while suffering from the vagaries of state politics during the war.

Blunt's reputation had been enhanced, or impugned, depending on the viewpoint of the observer, the fall before. At Little Town, now Oswego, Blunt presided over a court martial. Union soldiers had arrested all the important male citizens of the neighboring town of Chetopa and brought them to Little Town for trial on the charge of treason. They were charged with giving aid to the South.

Dr. George Lisle was the principal defendant in the court martial, and it was held in the cabin home of John Mathews after he had been killed by Federal soldiers from Fort Scott under Lieutenant Colonel Blunt. Blunt presided over the hearings, a young Kansas officer from Emporia, Preston B. Plumb, prosecuted, and William Alexander Johnson of Garnett handled the defense.

Dr. Lisle and the other defendants were acquitted but not without a considerable amount of intimidation by the Kansas soldiers trying them. This was the first session of any court of any kind held by white men in southeastern Kansas, but it did little to introduce law and order to that part of the young state. Instead, it established a precedent that led settlers later in the war to petition Gov. Samuel J. Crawford to locate the court and other offices of the Labette County seat in Oswego.

Blunt had been an officer in one of the regiments of the Lane Brigade and, as such, received political patronage from the senator. It was not long, however, before Blunt demonstrated that he was anything except Lane's puppet. For starters, Blunt—who had attended a military school in the East as a youngster—ceased the marauding style of fighting conducted by Lane's adherents in favor of a more formal type of warfare. Even though he was no less an abolitionist, Blunt gradually gained Lane's disdain. By the end of 1862, Blunt was a force to be contended with, and an open rift loomed between him and Lane.

Early in the spring of 1862, officials on the Kansas-Missouri border grew exasperated with the unabated depredations of the Lane Brigade and Jennison's Jayhawkers. Both General Halleck and Gen. David Hunter cast about for a way to bring the jayhawking under control. Initially, they grasped at straws. Rumors spread early in 1862, that a "Grand Army of the Southwest" was being organized in southeast Kansas.

The little town of Humboldt, twice raided by Missouri bushwhackers, was made headquarters for the 7th Kansas Cavalry to get them away from Missouri. The officers of the regiment, including Jennison and Anthony, were led to believe that they would march south as soon as weather permitted. To get to Humboldt from the Leavenworth and Kansas City areas, the regiment traveled over the miserable roads through sleet, snow, and ice, and the troopers took a week to cover just a hundred miles.

A letter from Lieutenant Colonel Anthony to his sister, Susan B. Anthony, made it clear that he believed the 7th Kansas was to participate in an army that would march through Arkansas to some distant objective such as New Orleans or perhaps even as far away as Galveston, Texas. This "newspaper expedition" never got beyond mere talk.

Late in March 1862, the 7th Kansas departed from Humboldt. Gen. David Hunter ordered the regiment to march north to Lawrence, then west through the new capital city of Topeka and on up the Kansas River valley to Fort Riley. Jennison's Jayhawkers were partly responsible for Humboldt's troubled history during the war. Missouri raiders associated Humboldt with the depredations of Jennison's rowdy regiment, and the small hamlet would be attacked by guerrillas three times before the end of the war.

Despite rarely being free of disciplinary problems, the 7th Kansas was not completely without control. In March 1862, Pvt. Alexander Driscoll of Company H was tried by court martial for desertion. He was convicted and shot to death by a firing squad. This was not Driscoll's first desertion—in fact, he already had a poor reputation when he enlisted in the Kansas regiment. He had already deserted from the British army during the Crimean War and from the Confederate army at the Battle of Lexington, Missouri.

He broke out of the stockade in which he was confined, ironically, for robbing a Unionist in Missouri, but more grievously for stabbing a fellow soldier of his own regiment. But the crime that most likely sealed his fate was his attempt to make his escape from the stockade on the expensive horse of the 7th Kansas's Lt. Col. Daniel R. Anthony. Even for Jayhawkers, this was going too far.

Also in February, Hunter placed all of Kansas under martial law in an attempt to control Jayhawkers. Gov. Charles Robinson, who had contended for months with these Kansans, wrote that they came together "ostensibly to operate against those who were reputed as lukewarm on the Union question, but really to rob every man of property."

By 1862, he had troops stationed in northeastern Kansas at the request of state Supreme Court Justice Samuel A. Kingman, who declared that the citizens of Kansas were as fearful of Jayhawkers as they were of Rebels from Missouri. Neither martial law nor Robinson's efforts checked the jayhawking. The governor told the 1862 state legislature that Kansas is "overrun with thieves and highway robbers." The governor's supporters blamed Senator Lane for openly supporting the raiders. Despite Hunter's martial law, which was retained later that year when James G. Blunt assumed command, the marauding continued unabated.

There was an election, that year of 1862, the first since Kansas had become a state, and Senator Lane faced two problems. One was his desire to depose Gov. Charles Robinson; the other was how to retain his military authority as a general while maintaining his seat in the U.S. Senate.

Lane seemed to solve the latter dilemma by employing his influence with President Lincoln and elsewhere in Washington to secure for Blunt a brigadier's commission and by mid-1862 command of the District of Kansas. Even though there were other Kansans far more qualified, as historian Albert Castel wrote, "Blunt was to all intents and purposes merely Lane in a different body and under a different name."

Senator Lane's political ascendance over Governor Robinson came about over the latter's ill-advised signature on some state bonds involved in fraud. Lane encouraged the state legislature to impeach Robinson. In February 1862, the state house of representatives agreed and a trial was set for June 16. Although resoundingly acquitted by the impeachment court, Robinson was never quite able to regain the trust of voters following the

"Bond Swindle." The edition of the Leavenworth *Daily Conservative* later said that "in politics Lane was the King."

Blunt quickly demonstrated that he could think for himself. He was assigned command of the District of Kansas on May 2, 1862. Lane's interest in controlling the military operations in Kansas had not only to do with his continued jayhawking but also with graft. Army supply contracts let by officers in the quartermaster and commissary bureaus under supervision of commanding generals made a great deal of money.

A commander who could control the awarding of contracts also stood to make large sums of money when cut in on the huge profits in return for obtaining contracts for the merchants, freighters, and speculators. Blunt shared with Lane in this graft. But he also maintained martial law to control Kansans raiding across the border, and he used Kansas regiments in more conventional warfare to wean them from jayhawking.

Among those regiments that were put to better use was the 7th Kansas Volunteer Cavalry. Maj. W.E. Prince received orders to assemble at Lawrence a planned brigade for duty in New Mexico Territory. This jury-rigged brigade was to include the 1st Kansas Infantry, the 12th and 13th Wisconsin Infantry regiments, and the 7th Kansas Cavalry already en route to Fort Riley. After a battle at Valverde, New Mexico Territory, Confederate forces withdrew back to Texas, and complaints of depredations by guerrilla bands in the Kansas City area caused the Federal troops to remain near the border.

Only the 2nd Kansas, now redesignated as a cavalry regiment, marched down the Santa Fe Trail to Fort Union, New Mexico Territory. The 2nd Kansas arrived to find the territory secure for the Union for the time being, and so the troops returned to Kansas, according to Capt. Samuel J. Crawford,

by way of Council Grove, Fort Riley, Topeka, and Lawrence to Fort Scott, Kansas[,] arriving there on the twentieth day of September, 1862; having traveled over two thousand miles from the day we broke camp near Kansas City on the twentieth of April.

In March 1862, after marching to Humboldt to get out of Missouri, soldiers of the 7th Kansas Cavalry Regiment were ordered to Fort Riley along with the 1st and 2nd Kansas and the 3rd Kansas Battery. While at Humboldt, there had been begun discussion of that grand march into the Trans-Mississippi Confederacy. But when the Kansans were sent to Fort Riley, they were intended to perform services against the Apaches, protect the Santa Fe Trail from both Confederates and Indians, and defend New Mexico Territory from invasion by Rebel Texans under Confederate Gen. H.H. Sibley.

Meanwhile, at Fort Riley, there was a report that Kansas soldiers destroyed the office of the *Kansas Frontier News,* allegedly a disloyal weekly newspaper published at nearby Junction City. More likely, the perpetrators were soldiers from the fort who were abolitionists from other Union states such as Iowa and Wisconsin. At the time of the report, no Kansas troops were yet stationed at Fort Riley.

The frontier fort had for a decade been a bellwether post in the factional politics dividing the United States. In addition to Union hero Nathaniel Lyons, many officers who now served the Confederacy had been stationed there, Robert E. Lee, J.E.B. Stuart, and Earl Van Dorn.

The influence of the Southerners was still felt in the eastern population center of Junction City, named for the confluence of the Kansas, or Kaw, River. Moreover, the *Kansas Frontier News* was published by a Democrat. The Yankee post commander apparently took no action against the soldiers involved in the sack of the supposedly secessionist newspaper.

Following the decisive Battle of Valverde, the units bound for Fort Riley were redeployed. From Fort Riley, the 1st Kansas and the 7th Kansas were sent to Mississippi. The 5th Kansas, part of Lane's Brigade, was reassigned and saw action with other conventional regiments in Missouri and Arkansas. Lane felt initially that Blunt would allow the status quo on the border, a logical assumption since the new general had been a lieutenant colonel in the 3rd Kansas, another regiment in the Lane Brigade.

With the military situation apparently under control, Lane began using his close ties to President Lincoln to encourage two other pet projects: recruiting Indian regiments and enlisting African-American troops.

Lane begged Lincoln to provide adequate protection for the southeastern and southern Kansas borders, requesting permission to organize the thousands of refugee Indian warriors. It had already been proven that Indian volunteer regiments could serve alongside white outfits when Confederate Indian regiments fought with the Southern army under Maj. Gen. Earl Van Dorn at the Battle of Pea Ridge, Arkansas, on March 7-8, 1862. Van Dorn was defeated by Union Maj. Gen. Samuel Curtis, Blunt's department commander, and pursued the retreating Confederates toward Little Rock, while Van Dorn moved remnants eastward to reinforce the Southern army near Shiloh. Thomas C. Hindman was sent to Arkansas to bolster the South's flagging hopes in that state.

Lincoln finally consented to Lane's urging to organize the Union Indians, and Col. William Weer of the 4th Kansas Volunteer Infantry was authorized to raise two Indian regiments, the 1st and 2nd Indian Home Guards. Weer's choice, like Blunt's before him, had a political rather than a military reason. Weer had been leader of the 4th Kansas, one of the Lane Brigade regiments, and part of the circle of radical abolitionists and Jayhawkers who followed Jim Lane.

He had been a lawyer from Wyandotte. He exhibited most of the qualities necessary for a successful military career under Lane: he had led a gang of Jayhawkers, he had stolen horses in Missouri, and he liked to drink.

In Kansas camps along the Fall River near Yates Center, Union Indians had been suffering severely from the cold and harsh winter weather. Many froze to death. Soon, too, disease

Col. William Weer was authorized to raise two Indian regiments.

broke out at the temporary shelters of the Creeks; many more died of sickness. Opothleyoholo met with Gen. David Hunter, who commanded the military department that included Kansas, to describe conditions in the Union Indian camps and the Indian Territory, spurring an interest in invading the territory and returning the refugees to their homes.

The 1st Regiment, under command of Col. Robert W. Furnas, was composed of Creeks and Seminoles who had fought under Opothleyoholo the previous winter. The 2nd Indian Regiment, commanded by Col. John Ritchie, consisted of a hodgepodge of tribesmen recruited from reservations and refugee camps throughout Kansas. Its members included Cherokees, Caddos, Delawares, Kaws, Kickapoos, Osages, Quapaws, and Shawnees.

Each company was composed of members from the same tribe, but even so, not all the 2nd Indian Regiment were friendly to one another. As Colonel Weer roamed southeastern Kansas organizing Union Indians, Confederate Gen. Albert Pike believed a Federal invasion of the Indian Territory was imminent.

General Pike's concern over a Federal invasion of Indian Territory was well-founded. By spring, Kansans were desperate to send the thousands of refugee Indians back to the Territory, while the Indians themselves wanted nothing more than to return to their homes. Weer's two Indian regiments were joined by parts of five whole regiments—the 2nd Ohio, some companies of the 6th Kansas Volunteers, a couple companies of the 10th Kansas, and the 9th Wisconsin Infantry, as well as two batteries of field pieces.

The elements of the white regiments congregated at Fort Scott. Hearing of a Rebel camp on Cowskin Prairie, a level area that extended down the Missouri-Arkansas border, they followed the leader of the makeshift brigade, Col. Charles Doubleday, as he invaded from the north.

The spring of 1862 saw one of pushes by both sides. In Virginia, General McClellan pushed up the peninsula to capture the Rebel capital of Richmond, only to be stymied by Robert E. Lee, who launched an offensive of his own north toward 2nd Manassas and Harper's Ferry. In Tennessee, General Grant captured Fort Henry and Fort Donelson, then started his envelopment of Vicksburg.

Later in the year, a Confederate invasion of Kentucky toward Louisville and Cincinnati by Braxton Bragg and Edmund Kirby-Smith attempted unsuccessfully to draw Grant away from the Mississippi River Valley. And in the Trans-Mississippi, Van Dorn's advance, which was stopped at Pea Ridge, was followed by an invasion into Arkansas by General Blunt's forces and the Indian Expedition under Colonel Weer.

Actually, Weer was still filling regimental rosters between the Kansas town of Leroy and the Osage Catholic Mission in Neosho County, Kansas, when the campaign into Indian Territory that General Pike had feared commenced. Not waiting for Weer's Indian regiments, Colonel Doubleday of the 2nd Ohio crossed the southern Kansas border with 2,500 men, including about 350 Kansans from the 6th and 10th Kansas Volunteers, to attack the secessionist camp at Cowskin Prairie. This was an area stretching east from the Grand River along the Missouri-Arkansas border. Doubleday's scouts found the Rebels about sundown on June 6, 1862.

It was dark by the time he had arranged about a thousand Yankees in line of battle and completely surprised Confederate Col. Stand Watie's 1st Cherokee Mounted Rifles and some Missouri irregular cavalry under Col. John T. Coffee. The artillery from Indiana opened the fray, followed by the drums of advancing massed infantry.

The Cherokees and Missourians had settled down to eat their evening meal, but upon the Union attack they abandoned tents and cooking fires in a mad scramble south. Although no casualties on either side were reported, morale among Doubleday's troops soared when they learned Stand Watie's Cherokees, reputed to be the premier Confederate Indian regiment, were the ones routed that night, and the

Confedcrates were alerted to the Federal invasion from the north.

After the fight at Cowskin Prairie, Colonel Weer ordered Doubleday to link up with the Indian regiments at Baxter Springs, where a Union post had been established across the border in Kansas. Then the combined commands pushed south into Indian Territory. On June 28, 1862, Weer's whites and Union Indians, as many as 6,000 men altogether, marched out of Baxter Springs. Pike had sent an urgent appeal to Major General Hindman for assistance, but Hindman was hard-pressed himself. He ultimately spared a battalion of Missouri cavalrymen under Col. J.J. Clarkson to help defend the Cherokee Nation and raid southern Kansas.

On July 3, Weer's troops, advancing through Indian Territory in two columns, struck not only Stand Watie's Cherokees but also Colonel Clarkson's Missouri cavalry. Along Spavinaw Creek, some of the 6th Kansas Cavalry surprised the 1st Cherokee. A desperate mounted battle ensued as the Southern Indians finally split into small groups to prevent the entire force from being crushed.

While some Kansans enjoyed success at Spavinaw Creek, members of the 9th Kansas Cavalry and the 1st Indian Home Guard attacked Clarkson's battalion of Missouri Rebels at day-break near the hamlet of Locust Grove. Clarkson believed there were no Union troops nearby, so his command, too, was totally surprised. In his nightshirt, Clarkson surrendered more than a hundred of his equally disrobed Rebs.

Some escaped when the first volleys raked the Rebel encampment, fleeing all the way to the Cherokee Nation. Upon word of the Yankee victories, modest as they may have been, some panicked and others switched sides. Enough of the latter volunteered for Colonel Weer to form yet another Kansas Indian regiment, the 3rd Indian Home Guard, with Col. William A. Phillips at its head.

On July 10, Weer marched his command farther south and sent a company of the 6th Kansas Cavalry and fifty soldiers of

the Indian Home Guards to seize Tahlequah, the capital of the
Cherokee Nation, and arrest Chief John Ross. Captain Harris
Greeno led the Federal command east to the Cherokee town.
Greeno's troops surrounded the place but learned that all the
adult males had departed.

After securing the town without firing a shot, Greeno next
found John Ross, principal chief of the Cherokees, at his plan-
tation outside Tahlequah. Ross surrendered, as did almost 200
Confederate Cherokees. Ross claimed his siding with the
South was owed to circumstances beyond his control, while the
troopers offered to join Greeno's Indian forces.

As Greeno was taking Tahlequah, Weer and another column
of some 800 men headed for the Arkansas River. There was a
brief skirmish at Fort Gibson, and then Weer pushed a few
miles south to the Arkansas, only to find Col. Douglas Cooper's
Choctaws and Chickasaws holding the far side of the river.
There were some desultory potshots before Weer withdrew all
the way back to where he had started.

Then he took to the bottle, and soon Col. Frederick
Salomon of the 9th Wisconsin and his brother officers
arrested Weer for intoxication. Leaving the Indian Home
Guard regiments—including the 3rd, which had been organized from among Cherokees in the Territory and was commanded by Col. William Phillips—in Tahlequah, the
expedition marched back to Fort Scott with nothing more
accomplished. Blunt was peeved that Salomon had abandoned so much enemy territory and Lane's Indian regiments,
not to mention leaving the southern border of Kansas protected by only three understrength, untrained, and in some
respects untested regiments. He planned a new invasion
with—amazingly—Weer in command.

In the meantime, Senator Lane beseeched Lincoln for per-
mission to fulfill his other pet project, raising African-
American troops. Once more the president acquiesced to
Lane's pressure. Charles R. Jennison was accused by one
Missourian of having a full company of African-Americans

under a black officer with him on a raid in Johnson County, Missouri, as early as November 1861.

James Montgomery from Fort Scott had been a leading proponent for recruiting African-Americans for more than a year. Late in 1862, he would visit numerous U.S. senators and even said he had enjoyed "a short interview with the President [Lincoln]." He would eventually be sent to the Deep South to organize the 1st South Carolina Volunteer Infantry, an African-American regiment. Now, however, Senator Lane began intensely recruiting his *Zouaves d'Afrique.* He threatened to use any opponents to his recruiting as cooks for the black regiments.

Of course, Lane had been gathering freed slaves before he received permission and despite the general hostility of most common Kansans. A handful of ardent abolitionists sought to "elevate" the African-Americans by putting muskets in their hands. In fact, the prejudice against black recruits was so intense that they had to be drilled in seclusion.

Even the African-Americans themselves were often reluctant recruits. On August 4, 1862, Lane declared "the negroes are mistaken if they think white men can fight for them while they stay at home. . . . We don't want to threaten, but we have been saying that you would fight, and if you won't fight we will make you."

To fill the ranks of the fourth regiment he raised, Lane resorted to various techniques. He offered pay of $10 per month and a "certificate of Freedom," even though white soldiers got paid more and the certificate held no value, since African-Americans in Kansas were already free.

Lane's recruiting officers were not even above kidnapping to fill out company rosters. On August 22, a gang of Jayhawkers crossed the border to Kansas City to "make converts" among the slaves. They gathered twenty-five black men and forty horses before a company of Union Missouri State Militia caught up to them, wounding one, capturing eight, and returning slaves and horses to their original places.

On October 28, 1862, some of Lane's African-American soldiers crossed into Missouri where they engaged in the first action of the Civil War between former slaves and their Southern oppressors when they fended off a force of Confederate irregulars around the town of Butler, Missouri. Federal patrols had been probing Bates, Vernon, Barton, and Jasper counties in Missouri along the Kansas line to hold secessionist raiders at arm's length.

Just outside the town of Butler in Bates County, elements of the 1st Kansas Colored Volunteers found a large party of the pro-Southern Missourians. In the short, noisy fight that followed, the African-American soldiers gave as good as they got, and they proved they could fight, demonstrating courage and discipline under hot fire. The battle at Butler confirmed the belief that former slaves were a valuable source of manpower among the ardent Kansas abolitionists.

Even among those fire-eaters there remained doubt about how the African-Americans would perform in combat. Some maintained that while the former slaves should be recruited and organized, they should be put to such tasks as teamsters, provost guards, and in labor battalions, leaving the real fighting to white soldiers. After all, only the black men who had run away from their masters and followed the Underground Railroad to free Kansas and points beyond had helped themselves. The rest had been freed by white abolitionists overthrowing the slavocracy in the nearby counties of Missouri.

Since it seemed to those naysayers that the freed slaves being enlisted in companies in Kansas had simply waited for white men to release them from bondage, then the new recruits should do what they did best—common labor—freeing white soldiers to continue the crusade and free even more of those in bondage.

A month after the battle at Butler, a battalion of African-American soldiers entered Missouri and showed that they could not only fight, but they could hold their own as Jayhawkers, too. Five companies of black soldiers marched out

Soldiers in Kansas regiments engaged in the first action between former slaves and their Southern oppressors.

of Fort Scott and crossed the border into Missouri at the town of Nevada. They were sent out to punish Confederate guerrillas and sympathizers in southwestern Missouri. Kansas officers could conceive of no greater humiliation for the slaveholding secessionists than to be brought the Kansas brand of justice by soldiers who had until recently been their bond servants.

At Island Mound, the African-American companies fought an even larger battle than at Butler. In cold, damp weather on November 28, 1862, the black men again performed with courage and discipline. A larger force of Rebel irregulars made a brief, concerted effort, fully expecting all the former slaves to break and flee like so many rabbits. They were met by sheets of flame and a hail storm of lead as the black troops stood shoulder to shoulder and fended off the attack with volley fire.

Gunsmoke and the clouds of the men's breath filled the air until the Missourians abandoned the field to the Federals. The victors of the Battle of Island Mound then collected a good share of booty, captured "a large amount of stock," and returned to Fort Scott in triumph. About the same time that autumn, Gen. Ben Butler enrolled three black regiments for the Union in New Orleans, Louisiana, but Kansas could justifiably claim to be the first Union state to enlist African-Americans and to test them in combat.

Lane made no effort to conceal his recruitment of blacks—indeed, he boasted far and wide of his success. His enrollment had barely commenced when outraged Missouri guerrillas struck back. On August 11, 1862, William Clarke Quantrill captured Independence, Missouri.

The success earned him a commission as captain in the Confederate Army, although he always had to recruit his own "regulators." He appointed George Todd and William Gregg his lieutenants. Todd had been a ne'er-do-well stone worker and ditch digger, while Gregg was a more intelligent and literate man, and had been a deputy sheriff of Jackson County.

Five days later, on August 16, a band of Confederate irregulars under Upton Hays attacked an equal number of Union

William Clarke Quantrill.

militiamen at Lone Jack, about 25 miles southwest of the scene of Quantrill's victory. After a desperate struggle in which about 125 men on both sides were killed in action, Hays called off his attack. He joined forces with Quantrill and the combined guerrilla commands headed south. While these two guerrilla successes did not invade Kansas, they would impact Kansans the next month.

Quantrill's and Hays's successes over Federal troops at Independence and Lone Jack rallied a large force from among the few men remaining in Arkansas to follow up these minor triumphs. John Schofield, the general commanding the Union District of Missouri, called for aid, and General Blunt with the 2nd, 6th, and 10th Kansas Volunteers were sent to head off the Confederates.

Throughout the summer Quantrill's reputation as a guerrilla leader grew with each victory. The numbers of his followers grew proportionately. They took their cue from their leader—they dressed in frilled shirts, rode blooded horses, carried multiple handguns, and fostered the aura of devil-may-care, frontier Robin Hoods.

Many were very young, almost too young to enlist in the volunteer regiments. Others had been cut off when secessionist Missourians fled to Arkansas. Still others had been Unionists who had switched sides after maltreatment by Jayhawkers. They followed Quantrill almost religiously, and they helped to make Quantrill's name one of the most feared on the border.

Upton Hays had also built a reputation, but one quite different from that of Quantrill. Whereas the latter became known for his brutality and for leading a ragtag band of erstwhile guerrillas, the former Santa Fe Trail trader Hays was a respected businessman viewed as driven to banditry by circumstances on the border.

He built an organization of more highly disciplined recruits who fought as a cohesive unit of irregulars and who had simply not had the opportunity to enlist, train, and drill earlier in the war. During 1861 and early 1862, Hays was acknowledged as a reputable leader by secessionist Missourians and as a formidable, honorable opponent by Unionist Missourians and Kansans.

Eight days after the fight at Lone Jack, on August 24, 1862, Maj. Gen. Thomas C. Hindman became Confederate commander of the District of Arkansas. Hindman soon learned of Quantrill's success at Independence and the fight Hays conducted at Lone Jack, as well as intelligence that the two had joined forces and were reported riding south. The new commander in Arkansas proposed joining them for a new attempt to secure control of Missouri for the Confederacy. He organized three regiments of exiled Missourians and put Col. Joseph O. Shelby in command of this brigade.

Hindman also called on Albert Pike, leader of the brigade of Confederate Indians, to bring his troops to augment the Southern force. Pike was disgruntled over the treatment of his Indian regiments, especially in terms of uniforms, weapons, artillery support, and supplies, so he reacted slowly. When Hindman repeated the order brusquely, Pike resigned.

Texas Col. Douglas Cooper, who had retreated ignominiously from Bird Creek in December 1861, promptly applied for Pike's job as Confederate Indian commissioner and brigadier general of volunteers. He moved the Rebel Indian brigade up the border between Arkansas and the Territory.

As September drew to a close, General Blunt led his Kansans in pursuit of the guerrillas. The 2nd, 6th, and 10th Kansas regiments caught up with the enemy and saw action around Newtonia, Missouri. So did the 9th Wisconsin and the 2nd Indian Home Guard regiments. On the road south Blunt was informed of Hindman's advance.

Col. John Ritchie's 2nd Indian Home Guard was among the first to skirmish with the Rebels. This was the Union Indian regiment that consisted of a variety of tribes. Some had been enemies in the past while others, especially the Osage, were hardly more than wild Indians. The regiment was more than Ritchie and his white officers could control, and near

Carthage, Missouri, the enlisted personnel behaved like poorly uniformed and even more poorly trained and disciplined Jayhawkers.

The citizens sought help from Shelby's brigade, so several Confederate companies of the 5th Missouri Cavalry led by Capt. Ben Elliott surrounded a camp of about 250 of the Indian soldiers on September 14 and surprised them. For two hours, Elliott's horse soldiers hunted down fleeing Indian soldiers in the heavily wooded area around Carthage, and some 200 new rifles that had been issued to the Indian Home Guard at Fort Scott were seized.

Ritchie's 2nd Indian Home Guard was the target again six days later when Col. T.C. Hawpe led his 31st Texas Cavalry and some local southwestern Missouri guerrillas organized by Maj. Tom Livingston somewhat north of Carthage at a crossing of the Spring River known as Shirley's Ford. With the first assault on Ritchie's camp came a rout of hundreds of women and children who traveled with the men of the command. Hawpe attempted to surround the Yankee Indians, and when this failed he launched a series of cavalry charges. After the initial surprise, the Union Indians stiffened their resistance.

Livingston suggested to Hawpe that the Southerners cut off the sizeable supply train, but the Texas colonel, aware of the nature of the border war, felt the wagons were too well protected. A major argument ensued, and Hawpe removed his Texans from the field. Livingston and his men took on hundreds of Indian troops alone. Battling against abruptly overwhelming odds, the surviving guerrillas barely escaped with their scalps.

After joining with Colonel Salomon's forces near Fort Scott, Blunt learned that Upton Hays, Jo Shelby, and Douglas Cooper had taken up a strong position behind tall stone walls in the fields surrounding the town of Newtonia, between Neosho and Springfield, Missouri. The Kansans attacked and in spite of the cover of the walls sent the Confederates flying in numerous directions.

Hays was killed in the Battle of Newtonia; Cooper fled with his Indians back to the Territory; Shelby retreated south down the road to northwest Arkansas's Boston Mountains; and Quantrill vanished into the bush.

Blunt brought the 2nd, 6th, and 10th Kansas regiments—which had met at Fort Scott with Colonel Salomon after Weer's expedition into Indian Territory—for the action around Newtonia. Now he led his Kansans in pursuit. They crossed the state line from Missouri and Arkansas to camp on the site of the Battle of Pea Ridge the previous March. Once there, Blunt received instructions from General Schofield to move his brigade, now designated the Army of the Frontier, to Old Fort Wayne. It was feared that Cooper's Confederate Indians would harass the Union supply lines, so Blunt's assignment was to soundly defeat them.

Leaving his first brigade under Salomon, now a brigadier general, at Pea Ridge, Blunt moved his other two brigades to the Arkansas-Indian Territory border. The army stopped at Bentonville, Arkansas, on October 21 just long enough to feed the men and horses. Then they pushed on in a forced march to attack Cooper's Confederates at Old Fort Wayne at day-break. The Yankee horse soldiers outdistanced the infantry, wagons, and artillery.

That night, the lengthy column stretched for miles along the Maysville Road, which led to Old Fort Wayne. When a brief rest stop was called, much of the weary army collapsed and fell asleep in their places. A short while later, Blunt and his staff started off again, but only part of the 2nd Kansas Cavalry rode out with him. The rest of the Army of the Frontier's 2nd and 3rd brigades remained asleep.

Oblivious to his lack of a following, Blunt pushed on until the wee hours of the morning. He stopped at an imposing farmstead to seek directions. The irascible, rotund little general personally disguised himself as a Confederate seeking to rejoin his regiment in Cooper's command. The lady of the house told him the Southerners were only about three miles

Blunt stopped at an unimposing
farmstead to seek directions.

west of the town of Maysville camped on the site of Old Fort Wayne. Sending two companies around the village to intercept any attempt to warn the sleeping Southerners, he rode to the rear of his column—a much shorter ride than he expected! He found only a single company of the 2nd Kansas.

Sending a courier with orders to bring all units to converge at the double quick, at dawn on October 22, Blunt audaciously chose to open the Battle of Old Fort Wayne by attacking Cooper's camp with just three companies of the 2nd Kansas. The surprised Confederates immediately assumed a defensive posture, permitting the Federals the opportunity to see assistance arrive to swell their ridiculously small attacking force.

The rest of the 2nd Kansas, along with a pair of mountain howitzers, showed up to open fire. An artillery duel raged in the early morning until Cooper realized his adversary's weakness and attempted a flank movement. Only the timely arrival of the 6th Kansas Cavalry and the 3rd Indian Home Guard thwarted the Rebel counterattack.

Blunt then ordered his entire force present to attack. Cooper's Texans and Confederate Indians retreated in disarray, and Kansans brought down the team drawing the Southern artillery. The 3rd Indian Home Guard and the 6th Kansas captured the Rebel field pieces and scattered Cooper's army like chaff in the wind, and the Battle of Old Fort Wayne came to an end.

With Shelby back deep in Arkansas and Cooper's force utterly disorganized and having vanished to the Territory, Blunt settled his army down for the winter. Another two divisions under young Brig. Gen. Frank Herron camped near the Wilson's Creek battlefield. Late in November, Blunt's scouts startled the camp with word that all of Hindman's cavalry— Shelby's Iron Brigade, the guerrillas routed at Newtonia, and other Missouri volunteers—were headed north yet again through the Boston Mountains. This time the Southerners were led by Brig. Gen. John Sappington Marmaduke, a dashing young Missouri horseman.

Blunt started south with the 2nd, 6th, 10th, and 11th Kansas regiments and the 3rd Indian Home Guards. He also had thirty cannon. He found Marmaduke on November 28, 1862, encamped at a tiny village called Cane Hill on the road between Fayetteville and Van Buren, Arkansas. The Confederate horse soldiers had hoped to winter in the lush valleys of orchards and farms, from which they could launch a campaign in the spring; instead, they were forced to fight a battle at Cane Hill.

The Yankees deployed quickly for battle. Blunt left Salomon with one division in reserve and ordered up the 11th Kansas under Col. Thomas J. Ewing, Jr., and the 10th Kansas under Weer (sober now). Right behind them was Colonel Phillips with the 3rd Indian Home Guard, and Lt. Col. L.R. Jewell's 6th Kansas.

For his part, Marmaduke drew Blunt's Kansans into a trap in the Boston Mountains. He planned to dismount his cavalrymen and fall back fighting through a narrow defile that restricted the firing lines so that the superior number of bluecoats would be all but ineffective.

Shelby commanded the retreat as his men arranged their companies so they could fire volleys at the advancing Federals, then retreat through their own lines. Thus Blunt was always confronted by a solid rank with loaded muskets. Shelby tried one counterattack but the Union line was just as solid as his own. For fifteen miles, the blue and gray ranks fought every foot of the way. As the Battle at Cane Hill ended, Marmaduke finally sent a flag of truce asking to gather his dead and succor the wounded.

Blunt granted permission, and asked who the commander of the opposition had been. He was told it was Shelby. A mutual respect arose between the Kansas abolitionist and the Missouri border ruffian. Blunt pulled out of the bloody valley even as Marmaduke and Shelby returned to the Boston Mountains.

Blunt tried again to settle in for the winter, this time at the village of Cane Hill, only to receive intelligence from his scouts and spies that Hindman was moving north yet again. His new army included Arkansas conscripts, the Indians Blunt had dispersed at Old Fort Wayne reinforced by Stand Watie's 1st Cherokee, and Shelby's Missourians, one of the largest congregations of Confederate troops in the Trans-Mississippi West during the entire war.

The safest tactic for Blunt to adopt would be a withdrawal to Herron's camp at Wilson's Creek. But Blunt had already proven his disdain for safety.

At Wilson's Creek, General Herron received an urgent telegram from Department Commander Samuel Curtis on December 3, 1862, relaying Blunt's request for reinforcements. Herron realized that the upcoming march would be grueling. He warned his troops that he expected them to make an epic march of about 125 miles without tents or equipment—even knapsacks would be hauled in wagons to follow the column. Hindman had to move his army—estimated to be as few as 15,000 or as many as 25,000 men—less than half the distance in the same amount of time. Even with the lowest of those numbers, the Southerners could conceivably overwhelm Blunt's troops.

Herron's men passed the Pea Ridge battleground on December 5. After midnight on December 6, the first companies of his reinforcing army reached Fayetteville. At the same time, Hindman explained to his Confederate officers that they must "chaw up Herron for breakfast, and then turn and gobble up Blunt at dinner."

To do this, a skeleton force of Rebels would maintain campfires and hold Blunt's attention with attacks and skirmishes. Then he would slip around Blunt's flank and his troops rush up the Fayetteville road searching for him to follow a tried and true method of war known as divide and conquer.

As did many Civil War battles, the Battle of Prairie Grove began accidentally. The van of Hindman's flanking Confederates led by Maj. David Shanks seized a Union commissary train on the Fayetteville road, driving off the troop of Federal Arkansas recruits with their revolvers. Hearing the fire in their rear, a Union Missouri regiment wheeled and drove off the Southerners. The rest of Herron's column struggled back to their weary feet and staggered down the road where, at about 7 A.M., they met the retreating Federal Arkansans.

Hindman definitely had the element of surprise on his side as Herron's troops straggled toward home on the morning of December 7. Instead of attacking, Hindman halted at Prairie Grove church along Illinois Creek and drew up in battle lines. He waited for Herron to attack, with Blunt's Yankee army only eight miles distant.

Hindman opened the formal battle with his artillery. Herron forded the creek with guns of his own and returned fire. After two hours of bombardment, Hindman ordered his troops to attack, but they were beaten off. He tried again, but a regiment of Arkansas conscripts deserted, so the general cancelled the attack. Herron then charged the Confederates twice, but the Rebel line did not budge. Herron worried about where Blunt was and why he did not join the fight.

The Battle of Prairie Grove opened
with an artillery duel.

At Cane Hill, Blunt still faced the skeleton force expecting an attack. When he heard the booming of artillery, he blurted, "My God, they're in our rear!" He led his forces personally to the fray and ordered his own field pieces to open fire. Hindman tried to intimidate him with a charge, but again the Arkansas conscripts failed, even though driven from behind by Marmaduke's cavalry. They could not face the grape and canister of Union artillery.

After an hour's cannonade, Blunt ordered a charge. Kansans crossed farmsteads to reach Southern lines. Hindman's left wing scampered for the woods, but Jo Shelby galloped his horsemen into the line to retake lost ground. The lines of both armies stood firm until darkness fell.

On the morning of December 8, Hindman requested a truce to tend the wounded and bury the dead, although he had already started to withdraw his army under the cover of darkness. Federal burial details reported that the Confederates were collecting fallen arms from the ghastly battlefield rather than picking up wounded men. Blunt demanded that this stop, and when some zealous Rebel parties persisted, he arrested them and sent them north with other prisoners of war. Churches and college buildings in Fayetteville became hospitals for the wounded, and Blunt's and Herron's forces rested briefly before heading south again.

Blunt had been fooled and surprised by Hindman at the Battle of Prairie Grove. Turnabout was fair play. Blunt surprised Hindman at Van Buren, Arkansas, and his enthusiastic Kansas cavalrymen chased the Rebs down the streets and out of town. Stopping at the Arkansas River at the edge of town, most of the Confederate supply wagons were captured and four steamboat loads of Southern quartermaster goods were burned. The Confederate state legislature of Arkansas downriver in Little Rock fled the Federal advance in panic.

But Blunt was now far from his base of operations, and his superior, the conservative John Schofield, was displeased about the battle at Prairie Grove and unhappy that the best troops in his command were so far from home base with over-extended supply lines. Schofield called him back.

Colonel Phillips, now in overall command of the Union Indian Brigade, also moved south to drive off Stand Watie and General Cooper. Phillips led his three Indian regiments, two companies of the 6th Kansas Cavalry, and a battery of four field pieces captured from Cooper at Old Fort Wayne and manned by volunteer gunners, into Indian Territory. He pushed into the Cherokee Nation and found Fort Gibson nearly abandoned.

However, across the Arkansas River a large force of Confederate Indians camped at Fort Davis, a post established by General Pike and named for the president of the Confederacy. Colonel Phillips approached on December 27, 1862. His inexperienced cannoneers fired on the Confederate flag flying in the brisk winter breeze, followed by a line of skirmishers.

A brief exchange of rifle fire ensued before the Cooper's warriors abandoned Fort Davis. Phillips ordered the post burned before pursuing Cooper and Watie into the Creek Nation, burning and pillaging the farms and homes of Southern sympathizers along the way in true Jayhawker fashion. But before Phillips caught up with his Confederate foes again, Schofield called him back, too.

As 1862 drew to a close, the Civil War in Kansas had become defined. The border war that had begun with jayhawking in 1861 had become a bloody guerrilla war and saw the rise of William Clarke Quantrill. The year also witnessed the success of Jim Lane in politics and the rise of James Blunt as a successful conventional commander. And during 1862 both African-Americans and American Indians were recruited into Kansas regiments. Some Kansans were sent east to fight in Tennessee, Kentucky, and Mississippi, but most served in Kansas, Missouri, Arkansas, and Indian Territory.

The years blended together seamlessly, with the action of December 1862, being followed swiftly by more of the same in 1863.

CHAPTER 3

"Courage, Stubbornness, and Determination": 1863

The year 1863 was to be one of decision for the Union armies—but it was hard to expect that it would turn out that way in January of that year.

The guerrilla war that resulted from the depredations of Jayhawkers would intensify to not only some of its most organized but also its most celebrated Southern accomplishments during 1863. A Kansas general would come into his own as a conventional army leader that year. Before the year was out, Kansans would lead African-American regiments on the border and also in other theaters of the war. Additionally, other Kansans led Indian regiments against Rebel Indians south of the Kansas border.

Elsewhere, Kansas regiments served in Tennessee, Kentucky, and Mississippi with larger armies and in some of the greatest battles of the war. On January 1, 1863, President Lincoln issued his Emancipation Proclamation, freeing the slaves in that part of the country not controlled by his Federal forces. But Kansas troops had already created their own methods of freeing slaves from Southern farms and plantations.

After nearly two years of war, some called for peace. In the East, draft riots took place, and peace Democrats, called Copperheads, called for an end to the fighting and even advocated letting the South go its own way. In Kansas, only a small minority, mostly Democrats, favored a conclusion to the fight-ing. In February 1863, the offices of the *Leavenworth Inquirer* were ransacked. The presses were smashed, the type was thrown into the street, and the typecases were burned.

The editor of the paper, Burrell F. Taylor, was a Democrat and had called a meeting of peace Democrats three days ear-lier. But it was disrupted by Radical Republicans led by Charles Jennison, rival editor Daniel R. Anthony, and notorious Jayhawker and leader of the Kansas "Red Legs" George Hoyt. Not intimidated, Taylor printed opinions advocating peace and had to be protected by armed city police and peace Democrats. On the night of February 9, the city marshal and several police-men, Anthony, and Democrats and Radical Republicans alike were embroiled in a shouting, shooting match.

At 9 A.M. on February 10, a large, excited crowd gathered outside the *Inquirer* office. Jennison mounted a box in front of the crowd to harangue the mob: "Yesterday, this establishment was a Printing Office, and I proposed to protect it—this morn-ing it is a *rebel fort,* and I propose to gut it!"

At that, the mob burst into the building "and in less than half an hour the whole establishment was a complete wreck." Editor Taylor took the better part of valor and shook the dust of Leavenworth from his boots.

Further south during that third spring of the war, both Kansas Federal troops and Missouri Confederate soldiers swept back and forth in northwest Arkansas and southwest Missouri. "The officers of the Confederate forces paid the Southern peo-ple in vouchers or Confederate money for supplies taken from them," recalled Union veteran and historian Wiley Britton,

> but the vouchers and Confederate money were worth-less when the Federal forces occupied the country. All supplies taken from the people by the Federal troops were or should have been receipted for by the officer taking them, the officer generally adding the remark to the receipt, "Payable on proof of loyalty," if the loyalty

of the party was regarded as questionable. The holders of these receipts could take them to the nearest quartermaster or commissary, and, on proper identification, obtain vouchers for them, and get the vouchers cashed at a slight discount by the nearest merchant or banker, provided the voucher did not contain the fatal remark, "Payable on proof of loyalty."

There was a justifiable fear early in the year that Rebel irregulars might attack wagon trains as far west in Kansas along the Santa Fe Trail as Council Grove, about a hundred miles southwest of the Missouri River towns on the border. Trade had dried up along that trail during the first two years of the war, but it gradually resumed, with Leavenworth serving as the eastern terminus for government and private freighters.

The freight carriers simply avoided the Kansas City area. They loaded goods destined for Santa Fe from the few steamboats arriving at Leavenworth, traveled southwest from the Federal fort and crossed the Kansas River at Lawrence. Some followed the military road west along the Kansas River to it source at the confluence of the Republican and Smoky Hill rivers at Fort Riley and joined the Santa Fe Trail many miles to the south. They returned east by one of the same routes to Leavenworth.

A few freighters under government contract apparently skirmished with Southern guerrillas in eastern Kansas west of Kansas City, but no accounts remain describing attacks on private freighters carrying nonmilitary goods.

The fear of Rebel bushwhackers was not only justifiable but also realized. In February 1863, George Todd, one of Quantrill's able followers, together with a strong band of marauders, plundered Spring Hill, in Johnson County southwest of Kansas City. Throughout most of April, as the weather warmed and the grass greened, residents all along the Santa Fe Trail in eastern Kansas noticed other unsavory characters riding west on the trail.

Eventually, a company of some forty irregulars joined forces under the leadership of Dick Yeager, another of Quantrill's ambitious lieutenants, near Council Grove in early May. At Diamond Springs, the first camping ground on the Santa Fe Trail west of Council Grove, the gang looted a store and murdered its Unionist owner. A posse of volunteers attacked the raiders along the Cottonwood River, capturing ten and scattering the rest. The prisoners were turned over to a company of Kansas soldiers and later were all shot "while attempting to escape."

Yeager and the stragglers rode slowly eastward on the trail, killing or wounding several men, holding up a stagecoach, and ransacking the villages of Black Jack and Gardner in Johnson County near the state line before crossing the border back into Missouri.

Meanwhile, according to a member of the posse that pursued the guerrillas, "Quite a number of secesh sympathizers in and around Council Grove gave bonds for their good behavior in the future and took the oath of allegiance." Even so, one man was seized in Council Grove "for treasonable utterances, spitting on the U.S. flag, &c.," and was shot.

Also in May, another band of newly commissioned Confederate officers suffered an even worse fate. Charley Harrison, the noted gunman from Arkansas who had become the self-appointed leader of those Southern sympathizers called Bummers in Denver, Colorado Territory, decided his followers needed more legitimacy. Almost a third of the gold rush boomtown's population was from the South. In the spring of 1863, he and about twenty of his boys rode south to pick up a branch of the Santa Fe Trail at Big Timbers in Colorado Territory and then headed east on the trail to the nearest organized Confederate army in Harrison's home state of Arkansas.

These men sought commissions from some Confederate higher command to legitimize their organization of the large number of Southerners in Colorado and seize the gold works for the South . . . or stir up war among the Plains Indians . . . or open a new theater to draw Federal troops away for the Eastern fronts . . . or perhaps for a combination of these reasons.

An even more likely possibility was that Harrison and his bummers desired personal gain and position in Colorado Territory in the event that the war ended favorably for the South.

Mid-May arrived before Harrison secured his men commissions—perhaps from General Sterling "Old Pap" Price—and could head back to Colorado Territory. From Price's headquarters in Arkansas, the intrepid band crossed southwest Missouri and entered southeastern Kansas, cautiously avoiding contacts with any Yankee patrols.

Once past the settled parts of southern Kansas, they felt safe enough to ride openly in a beeline for the Santa Fe Trail, cutting it near the Great Bend of the Arkansas River. All that was between them and their colleagues in Denver were a few Indians, and the Coloradans had shown them how white Southerners dealt with their kind on the way east.

The Osage, disliking trespassers on their reserve, argued with some of Harrison's party. Some said the Indians wanted to take the whites to the nearest Union garrison for identification. In the heated exchange that followed, someone shot one of the Osage.

The Osage who inhabited southeastern Kansas were considerably different from the Southern Cheyenne, the Arapaho, and the Utes with whom Harrison's little force were familiar. The tall, handsome warriors with roached hair had been pressed by civilization for generations. They had been pushed west from their homeland along the Mississippi River at first contact with whites to the prairies and plains of Kansas.

The Colorado guerrillas behaved as their own usual brash, boorish, and cavalier selves on the way east, deeply offending the Osage, who were little more than wild Indians. The warriors eagerly awaited their return and a chance to even the score. Their opportunity arose as the new Confederate officers approached the banks of the Verdigris River in southeast Kansas. About 150 Osage under a chieftain named Hard Rope caught up to Harrison's horsemen and fired, killing one. They were driven back. But since some Osage were armed with long-range trade rifles while the Coloradans had mainly sidearms, Harrison's men fled for the protection of the steep river banks. It became a running battle.

Even the shelter of the streambed was an inadequate defense against the overwhelming numbers of the still-wild Indians. Two Osage who knew some of their tribe in the 2nd Indian Home Guard showed up in Humboldt to report the massacre of the white men. All but two of Harrison's party were found by members of the 9th Kansas Cavalry, stripped, scalped, and mutilated. Harrison, who was balding, had his luxurious beard scalped from his chin instead of having a top knot scalped from his head.

Two men escaped to relate the events. One was Warner Lewis, a relative of explorer Merriweather Lewis. The two men believed their luck had run out when they had fallen behind in the race for life, according to their story. Much to the contrary, the Osage somehow had bypassed them, making that their good luck day.

The pair of men concealed themselves under the Verdigris riverbank until dark. Then, with only the stars to guide them, they walked over the prairie, across the Osage Reserve, past the Federal outposts along the line to discourage irregular activity, into Missouri, and finally to Confederate lines in Arkansas. There they shared their side of the story.

Some writers discuss Harrison's mission as following orders from the Confederate general commanding Arkansas, Theophilus Holmes, to incite Plains Indians to take the warpath against Union forts and roads and settlers in western Kansas. Others have insisted that both Harrison and Yeager were caught deep in Kansas as part of a plan to draw Kansas troops away from the border or from protecting Lawrence, the

second largest city in Kansas at that time and known throughout the country as the seat of abolition.

There is a third possibility, although no documentation sup-
ports it. During the spring and summer of 1863, Southern
guerrillas ransacked Kansas. In September, Col. Joseph O.
Shelby, a ballot-box stuffer during "bleeding Kansas," who converted from a border ruffian to a conventional Confederate
officer, led a major cavalry raid throughout central Missouri.
Further east, Union Gen. Ulysses S. Grant was closing on
Vicksburg, the last stronghold of the South on the Mississippi
River.

Still further east, Gen. Robert E. Lee prepared to lead his
Rebel Army of Northern Virginia in an invasion of the Union
around Washington, D.C. The increasing guerrilla activity and
raiding in the Trans-Mississippi West might have been attempts
to draw Federal forces away from the defense of the nation's
capital or alternately from the drive to seize the length of the
country's most important river.

But if that was not the reason for the concerted effort, there
may have been some coordination among the bushwhackers in
support of Jo Shelby's Missouri raid, which occurred in
September 1863. Regardless of the reasons for Rebel irregulars
striking deep inside Kansas and crossing to the front range of
the Rocky Mountains, the result was a new year of terror
among Kansas citizens leading to the climax of the guerrilla
war on the Kansas-Missouri border.

Had Harrison indeed been sent to arouse the Plains tribes?
It is just as likely that Federals concocted that excuse to lay
blame at the Confederate doorstep while avoiding the responsibility for bringing on the Indian war that ignited on the
plains the next spring. In fact, before the war and early in the
conflict, frontier settlers often got along well with the Native
Americans.

For example, Christina Phillips was the only white woman in
the westernmost Kansas town, Salina. While her menfolk were
gone during the war, Mrs. Phillips minded their store and

traded with Plains Indians for pelts, robes, and furs. The Indians called her "White Sister," and they respected her. She never sold them alcohol, never traded on Sunday, and although patient with them, was always firm and honest.

She had squaws laugh at her white behavior till "tears rolled down their cheeks"; chased off drunken Wisconsin or Iowa soldiers at gunpoint when they chased two Kansa Indian men into her house for refuge; and treated an Indian woman who was "heap sick" with a dose of castor oil, only to have her husband announce, "Heap good medicine, two papoose."

Knowing the Plains natives as they did, some Kansans on the frontier were critical of the policies pursued by those representing the Federal government. Since any documents Harrison's luckless band might have carried conveniently disappeared, it was easy to blame those who were dead and on the losing side of inflaming the frontier. The guerrilla war in eastern Kansas peaked during the summer of 1863, but the guerrilla fighting on the frontier was only about to begin.

Guerrillas were the greatest threat to Kansas during 1863, but they were not the only problem with which commanders of the District of Kansas had to contend, nor did the threat of Missouri regulators slow some Kansans from pursuing their personal or business interests. In 1863, Indian tribes still held great parcels of Kansas land, much of it in reservations for those tribes removed from the east in the 1830s and 1840s.

White settlers who followed them some two decades later complained that the presence of the Eastern Indian reservations retarded the progress of Caucasian civilization. Some claimed that the Federal government owed it to the state of Kansas to put an end to the Indian title to lands completely. The government had elsewhere been in the habit of extinguishing Indian claims to gain concessions for traders, land speculators, and railroad companies.

Even though no track was laid, railroad speculation was rampant during the war. As early as 1862, a railroad company—the Leavenworth, Pawnee, and Western—had a treaty drawn up that was intended to undermine tribal cohesion and make way for government subsidies and land grants. The railroad company officials were dismayed to find Potawatomi tribesmen claiming the best timbered lands along the railroad's planned right of way.

Even a year before, it had seemed that the only solution for the ambitious civilians might be the removal of the Potawatomi to Indian Territory—at a time when the Federal government, and especially the new Kansas government, could not even return refugees from the territory to their homes! Now, in 1863, some Kansans contended that the Indians should forfeit their land claims entirely, even if it required Kansas troops to move onto the reservations to provide the seeds of white town settlement. They were ready to coerce the Potawatomi and other tribes to give up their land and to become civilized or be removed by military force to the Indian Territory.

The intensification of guerrilla fighting on the border, policing Indian reservations, and arguing with altruistic civilians fell into the bailiwick of Brig. Gen. James G. Blunt, commanding the District of Kansas. Early 1863 saw so much activity to occupy Blunt's attention that his organizational and logistical skills were tested to their fullest. In addition to dealing with the bushwhackers, the Kansas general was called upon for reinforcements by Col. William Phillips, now commander of the Kansas Union Indian Brigade at Fort Gibson, replacing the inebriated Col. William Weer.

The small number of forces under Colonel Phillips were being pressed by Confederate Indians and Texans under Gen. Douglas Cooper. Additionally, Indian tribes who still held reservations amounting to four million acres in Kansas called for help from Blunt's military office to control white squatters on their Kansas reserves. Meanwhile, settlers complained to Blunt that their neighborhoods were about to crack under "the oppressive load" of new arrivals and demanded troops to clear the Indians from the land for white settlement.

Even conventional Confederate volunteer cavalry and

infantry such as that under Jo Shelby threatened Blunt's district. All these demands on his few available forces, combined with strain upon supplies, troops, and equipment, caused the general deep concern about whether he could maintain control of southeastern Kansas.

Blunt's solution to the bushwhacker problem was simply to adopt a policy of grandiose public executions in an attempt to punish guerrillas while at the same time placating loyalists. Guerrilla chiefs such as Quantrill, Hayes, and similar irregular leaders tried for a short while to exchange prisoners, but Blunt remained firm. He adamantly insisted that "all persons known to be in arms against the Federal authorities of this District, will be summarily put to death when captured."

Finally, after even further escalation of the cycle of attack, counterattack, and revenge, in which guerrillas led by George Todd captured a Union wagon train and killed fourteen Federal troops, a new department commander, Gen. John M. Schofield, split Blunt's district into two parts. Blunt controlled the southern half with headquarters at Fort Scott. Gen. Thomas Ewing, Jr., commanded the northern half from Kansas City.

Schofield was one of the young Kansans to achieve tremendous responsibility. At age 32, he found himself in charge of more than 40,000 men in his department. He promptly sent half of them east to Grant at Vicksburg; most of them were from Missouri, but now there were far fewer troops to occupy the guerrilla-infested neighboring state.

Schofield recognized the natural pincer he had with Phillips and the Union Indian Brigade at Fort Gibson, Indian Territory, and a strong force at Helena on either side of Little Rock, capital of Confederate Arkansas. But while Schofield saw a way to secure Missouri and capture the capital—which might even knock Arkansas out of the war—he did not reckon with the opposition of Radical Republicans. They accused him of being too lenient with traitors and even of being in collusion with the pro-Southern guerrillas. They appealed to Jim Lane, the most powerful of their number.

Blunt was still viewed as a political general in Lane's camp by most higher-ranking officers. Even though Blunt showed clear signs of thinking for himself and had acted effectively at Cane Hill and Prairie Grove, he remained a hard-nosed abolitionist and staunch Radical Republican. Blunt considered his removal to the southern portion of Kansas—where he had control of the forces in Indian Territory and in southwest Missouri as well as Kansas—to the plains to be a punishment.

That may well have been part of the reason. But in light of Yeager's raid near Council Grove and Harrison's demise on the Verdigris, along with growing unrest among the Southern Cheyenne and the Arapahoe, there was cause for concern about keeping the lines of communication along the Santa Fe Trail open. And despite the change in command, the bush-whackers were no more under control with Ewing in command that they had been under Blunt.

If anything, the guerrilla war intensified. And even as Kansas forces contended with irregulars along the border, Colonel Phillips and the Indian Brigade faced strong opposition in Indian Territory.

On May 19, five Confederate regiments under Gen. Douglas Cooper crossed the Arkansas River, and at 9 A.M. the following morning they advanced to within two miles of Fort Gibson. Colonel Phillips' Kansas white cavalry and Indian regiments sprang into action and soon filled entrenchments as two battalions of Indians and a section of the 3rd Kansas Light artillery advanced. A clash with Cooper's Confederate Texans and Indians a mile from the fort cost about twenty killed and twenty wounded on each side, but Fort Gibson remained in Union hands. Nevertheless, Phillips and his garrison were besieged and cut off from the nearest Federal units.

A mixed command from regiments from Colorado, Wisconsin, and Kansas along with a section of the 2nd Kansas Light Artillery escorted about 300 army wagons in relief of Phillips at Fort Gibson. About halfway from Fort Scott to Fort Gibson lay a small Union outpost at the village of Baxter

Springs where the column was joined by a newly formed Federal regiment, the 1st Kansas Colored Infantry commanded by Col. James M. Williams.

It was also met at Baxter Springs by an escort dispatched by Colonel Phillips consisting of parts of each of the three Indian regiments and the 6th Kansas Cavalry under Maj. John Forman of the 3rd Indian Home Guard. The reinforced column and wagon train headed out of Baxter Springs on the Fort Scott to Fort Gibson military road, but a Yankee force this large could not long avoid notice by Rebel scouts—especially the Confederate Indian scouts.

They kept Cherokee Col. Stand Watie informed of the relief column's southward movement. Watie planned a surprise attack at the ford of the military road across Cabin Creek, but some Union Cherokees discovered the trap. Heavy rain and high water slowed the Federal column's progress, allowing the Yankee leaders time to plan the upcoming fight. Leaving the 6th Kansas Cavalry to protect the circled wagons, the rest of the combined forces advanced to the ford on the hot, muggy July 2, the same day armies faced each other at Gettysburg and along the Mississippi at Vicksburg.

The Kansas artillerymen fired a half-hour cannonade before Major Foreman led a company of Union Indian horsemen in a charge across the bank-full creek. The Federal riflemen lined the banks to provide a withering covering fire as the 9th Kansas Cavalry attempted to duplicate the assault by their Indian colleagues. They gained a tentative foothold on the Rebel-held bank.

Next, Colonel Williams led his African-American regiment in a gallant infantry attack. They held their rifles over their heads as they struggled through the waist-deep stream, then rushed in a headlong dash into the brush that lined Cabin Creek amid a hail of bullets from Rebel rifle pits. Against such a display of determination and grit, Watie's lines collapsed and his men fled. Some drowned trying to swim the flooding Grand River. Federal losses amounted to three dead and thirty wounded, but Southern losses were unknown.

The train and its escorts arrived safely at Fort Gibson two days later. Of major significance at the Battle of Cabin Creek was the performance of the 1st Kansas Colored Infantry in the first major action of African-American soldiers in the Civil War. They proved that black troops could fight just as well as white soldiers.

As early as April 2, 1863, Secretary of War William Stanton had received a telegram that Gen. Samuel R. Curtis had "a well drilled regiment of blacks at Fort Leavenworth." This was the 1st Kansas Colored Volunteers commanded by Col. James Williams, and they were soon performing garrison and fatigue duty at or near Fort Scott. The telegram was sent by U.S. Adjutant General Lorenzo Thomas, who opined that if the 1st Kansas Colored Infantry regiment "could be sent on the Mississippi [River] it would have a good effect upon the contrabands and facilitate enlistments." Thomas was a strong proponent of new regiments of African-Americans to protect freed slaves and others along the Mississippi.

Kansans had been proponents of African-American soldiers from the outset of the war, but in 1863 they saw their efforts rewarded with success. On January 13, Col. James Montgomery was authorized by the Federal War Department "to raise, subject to the approval of the general commanding the Department of the South and under his direction, a regiment of South Carolina volunteer infantry, to be recruited in that State, to serve for three years or during the war."

The Kansan from Fort Scott had been a leading advocate for recruiting freed slaves during his jayhawking days early in the war. Late in 1862, he visited with numerous influential U.S. senators and even had "a short interview with the President [Lincoln]."

The channels through which he operated his one-man lobby were complicated, but the results of his efforts became clear when his authorization arrived. In less than a fortnight the organization of the 1st South Carolina Volunteer Infantry Regiment was complete, and included African-American enlisted men, with volunteer white officers. Additionally, recruiters "commenced the organization of the 2nd [Colored] Regiment, which is to be commanded by Colonel Montgomery."

Also in early 1863, work was afoot to create an outfit unique in the annals of the war. An independent artillery battery was raised at Leavenworth from among freed slaves. Contrary to traditional organization of "colored" units mustered during the war, in this battery all three of the officers were also African Americans. The captain, organizer, and chief recruiter was H. Ford Douglass. W. D. Matthews was first lieutenant, and Patrick H. Miner was second lieutenant.

Captain Douglass was already a veteran. He was one of the earliest African-American soldiers to enlist in the Union Army. He served in Company G, 95th Illinois Volunteer Infantry Regiment in 1862. He even wrote to Frederick Douglass, the most noted and revered black in the United States, urging the elder statesman to follow his soldiers' example and "lay down the quill and take up the sword."

Both the enlisted men and battery's officers suffered from racial discrimination by white Kansas soldiers. So did other black regiments. Among the arguments often made was that since the former slaves had no previous military heritage and were an unknown quantity, they would not be effective fighters against Southerners, some of whom had been slaveholders.

The decisive victory of the 1st Kansas Colored Volunteers at Cabin Creek proved not only that they would fight but also that they would fight well. If fact, the ex-slaves filling the ranks of "colored" regiments were told by their white officers and believed that they had to fight hard because the only alternatives they faced in battle were victory or death. They could expect no sympathy as fellow soldiers or any quarter from the Confederate forces.

While a majority of Kansas soldiers served in their own state or in neighboring vicinities such as Missouri, Arkansas, and the Indian Territory, some regiments and individuals found themselves elsewhere. Colonel Montgomery left Kansas for

Washington, D.C., and then commanded his black regiments in South Carolina and Florida. Gen. Robert Mitchell, who had been promoted to brigadier at the same time as Blunt in 1862, commanded Union troops in Kentucky and in 1863 participated in the campaign to capture Vicksburg.

The 1st Kansas Infantry was stationed at Lake Providence, Louisiana, and the men of the regiment were in for a surprise. When one of their fellows died and was laid out for burial, they discovered the soldier was a woman.

"She was brave as a lion," said one 1st Kansas soldier. "She was a Sergeant when she died . . . [and] would have been promoted to a Lieutenancy in a few days if she had lived."

And the unruly 7th Kansas Volunteers—"Jennison's Jayhawkers"—were in Somerville, Mississippi, in January, 1863, and in a full-fledged, murderous mutiny. Members of Company B liberated a cache of liquor among Confederate "commissary stores," and the whole company from captain to lowest private liberally imbibed.

The company commander had posted guards to protect the whiskey, but when persistent troopers tried to bypass them, the captain berated them and threatened to shoot them while the men were on parade. A melee and a mad chase on horseback involving the captain and one of the fleeing enlisted men resulted in the death of both, and the remainder of Company B were severely disciplined for weeks after the brief, inebriated mutiny.

The rest of the 7th Kansas took the results to heart, but change was difficult. A month later, when the regiment was in Tuscumbia, Alabama, one of the soldiers wrote home deploring the absence of religious services: "No Meeting and no Chaplain and Sunday often passes without our knowing it." He wrote later, "There is a great deal of vice and wickedness. . . . For soldiering is a very bad school."

Although there were conflicting reports about religious convictions of Kansans, there was little doubt about the morals of the men in the army. Possibly the indifference to religion merely reflected the youthfulness of the soldiers. When the war broke out, nearly 90 percent of Kansans were under 40 years of age, and over 40 percent were between 20 and 40. Anyone beyond 40 usually had the word "Old" attached before his name when referred to by others. These young men would become targets of evangelists in revivals as the war dragged on.

Up in Tennessee, the 8th Kansas Infantry spent six months in Nashville doing provost duty. In June, the regiment moved to Murfreesboro to join the Union army under Gen. William S. Rosecrans in its drive to take Chattanooga. The 8th fought at Shelbyville, then marched to Winchester near the Tennessee River. The entire Federal army was brutalized on September 19-20 at Chickamauga, in which the 8th Kansas was a significant participant.

The Battle of Chicakmauga was the culmination of action by General Rosecrans' Army of the Cumberland against Gen. Braxton Bragg's Confederate Army of Tennessee in which the important railway center at the city of Chattanooga, Tennessee, was captured. Rosecrans tried to defend the city while outflanking Bragg's Southerners to force them out of Tennessee.

On September 19, the Confederate army, reinforced by Rebels from the Army of Northern Virginia under Gen. James Longstreet, launched an attack to recapture Chattanooga. The 8th Kansas under Col. John A. Martin of Leavenworth was in Heg's brigade of the XX Corps of the Army of the Cumberland.

On the late morning of September 19, the brigade moved into line of battle in some woods near Rosecrans' headquarters south of Chattanooga along the Chickamauga River. Moving up only some 100 yards, the 8th Kansas and a Wisconsin and two Illinois regiments encountered blistering fire from Rebel troops who had taken position along a roadbed. Col. Hans Heg, the brigade commander, was mortally wounded, so Martin assumed command.

A seesaw fight ensued through the forests and mountains of

southeast Tennessee. With the 8th Kansas in the thick of it, the brigade fell back, then counterattacked, only to be forced back by the Southerners again. The day's fighting ended with the 8th Kansas in virtually the same position from which they started about 11:30 that morning.

Ordered to support Gen. Phil Sheridan's 3rd Division, Martin's brigade advanced across the road in front of them to a small barricade and a ravine when "the enemy rose up from the tall weeds in front of us and advanced on us four columns deep, pouring in a destructive fire." Flanked on their left and outnumbered in front, the brigade fell back, rallied briefly some 200 yards from their original position, then was totally routed as the Confederates pressed their advantage.

Finally, near Rosecrans' former headquarters the remains of the regiments rallied, but in the meantime suffering almost 60 percent casualties, which, Martin wrote "amply attests the courage, stubbornness, and determination with which the troops fought." The 8th Kansas at Chickamauga had over 400 men from the state engaged. There were 2 officers and 28 enlisted men killed, 9 officers and 158 enlisted men wounded, and 25 enlisted men missing or captured—a total of 220 losses.

Nearly a year after the war ended, the names of five Kansas soldiers who were buried at Andersonville were released to the Kansas press. These men were members of the 8th Kansas who had been captured at Chickamauga and incarcerated in that Confederate prison camp. Captured Federals were sent to this most notorious of Southern prisons. Hundreds of the prisoners of war died there of malnutrition, disease, and exposure while awaiting parole or exchange; they were buried in haste at Andersonville. Almost a year after the South surrendered, remains of Federal soldiers were being exhumed and identified.

The names of the men from the 8th Kansas were released after considerable identification procedures, and their families were pleased to finally know what had happened to these soldiers. Few other Kansas officers found themselves locked away

*The 8th Kansas Volunteers were in the thick
of the Battle of Chickamauga.*

at Andersonville because of the distance from the other theaters where Kansans served. Regardless, many Kansans were
incensed to learn that their brethren had died there.

The 8th Kansas fared better, and in some eyes redeemed
itself, later that fall. In November, the Union army at
Chattanooga had licked its wounds and prepared to move
south. Blocking its way was the Confederate army ringing the
city on the heights of Missionary Ridge and Lookout
Mountain. On November 25, 1863, the 8th Kansas moved from
a railroad line near Fort Wood outside Chattanooga as skirmishers for Martin's brigade.

It supported the brigade, moving out about 2 P.M. to capture
some high ground, and seized a line of fieldworks against min-
imal resistance before the rest of the Union army advanced.
The 8th Kansas held that position for approximately an hour
until 3 P.M., when it moved with the rest of its brigade to assault
the Confederate works at the foot of Missionary Ridge.

Kansans were more successful in the Trans-Mississippi West.
In Arkansas, the elderly Rebel Gen. Theophilus Holmes sus-
pected that the overstretched lines from Kansas to Fort Gibson
and the guerrilla warfare rife along the Kansas-Missouri border
presented a chance to reestablish Confederate control of that
Southern state. If he could recapture Helena and drive the
Union Indians, African-Americans, and Kansans out of Fort
Gibson, he would control the Arkansas River and the rich agricultural southern half of Arkansas.

Such a victory would also draw off some of the Federal
troops besieging Vicksburg. Holmes proposed to strike at
Helena in late June or early July with a brigade of Arkansas
infantry, Sterling Price's Missourians, and Gen. John S.
Marmaduke's Missouri cavalry, including Jo Shelby's Missouri
Confederate Iron Brigade.

The advance on Helena, defended in part by Kansas troops,
took place on July 4, 1863, the day that Lee began his withdrawal from bloody Gettysburg and John C. Pemberton surrendered Vicksburg. Almost 8,000 Rebels attacked some 4,000

Federals and were defeated after desperate fighting, with an astonishing 1,600 casualties. Holmes fell back and fortified Little Rock, the Arkansas state capital, to little avail. The Southern losses at Gettysburg, Vicksburg, Helena, and Cabin Creek left the Trans-Mississippi West Department completely cut off from the rest of the Confederacy.

Following the debacles at Cabin Creek and Helena, the command of the Trans-Mississippi West Confederacy fell to the elderly Holmes' able assistant, Maj. Gen. Edmund Kirby-Smith. The new Southern commander determined to salvage a semblance of victory from the dual defeats with a sudden counterstrike—the only instance of offensive action in the entire Confederacy in July 1863.

Kirby-Smith rallied some Arkansas troops, Stand Watie's hard-riding horsemen, and Cooper's Chickasaw and Choctaw regiments, Texans, and batteries. They were ordered to rendezvous at Honey Springs, a hamlet on the Texas Road from Missouri through Indian Territory some 18 miles below Fort Gibson.

At the fort, Blunt learned of the Rebel concentration. Always aggressive and ready for action, he gathered his African-Americans, Phillips' Indian Brigade, and some companies of the 6th Kansas Cavalry, the 2nd Colorado, and the 3rd Wisconsin. Although the Confederates outnumbered his force by nearly two to one, Blunt's men were better armed, had better powder, and had a dozen artillery pieces. Honey Springs was the most important Confederate outpost in the Indian Territory and represented a threat to Fort Gibson, so Blunt saw an opportunity to secure his precarious hold in the territory.

At dawn on July 17, the 6th Kansas Cavalry clashed with about 500 Rebel horsemen, chasing them south from the field. It was about eight o'clock that morning when Blunt's smaller Federal force came upon Cooper's Confederates drawn up in a line of battle along the north bank of Elk Creek. Blunt rested his men, even allowing them breakfast from their field packs. During a well-deserved hour and a half break, Blunt, Col.

William R. Judson of the 6th Kansas, Colonel Phillips, and some staff officers scouted Cooper's position till they drew fire from sharpshooters and a brief but heavy thunderstorm cooled both sides.

Blunt organized a cavalry column under Judson consisting of his regiment, the 1st Indian Home Guard, and the 2nd Colorado on the right wing and an infantry column under Phillips consisting of his 2nd Indian Home Guard, the 1st Kansas Colored Infantry, and the 3rd Wisconsin on the left. Battle flags were uncased, drummers stroked the taut heads of their instruments, and men cheered as both columns stepped out lively and confident.

A short, one-sided artillery duel blasted away, with the Rebel cannoneers proving surprisingly accurate, landing shells among a clutch of Yankee officers, killing one of Blunt's aides. In a seesaw, four-hour fight, the Union Indian and black troops, along with the hard-working 6th Kansas, wore down the Rebels. Men of the 2nd Indian Home Guard advanced too far too fast and exposed themselves to the fire of the rest of the Union line.

When the Federal fire slackened to allow the 2nd Indian to fall back to where they belonged, the Confederate 29th Texas Cavalry assumed the Union line was about to fold. The Texans advanced on foot to take advantage of the confusion, but they failed to detect the 1st Kansas Colored Infantry concealed by black powder smoke and tall prairie grass. The black soldiers had crept quietly through the tall grass prairie to support the Federal flank.

They took the first Texans before they knew what happened or could sound an alarm, then rose from their concealment and raked the Confederates with volley fire. The Southerners came alert, men screaming and cursing, racing to escape the unplanned trap, some dropping their weapons, others falling wounded and dead in mid-stride.

Even though their commander had been severely wounded and carried from the field, the African-American soldiers fired two volleys point-blank into the Texans, causing them to flee in disarray. An infantry assault was mounted in the midst of the confusion, dooming the Texans' counterattack that was cut to pieces as it charged across the prairie after the retreating Kansas Indian soldiers.

Seeing the rout, the entire Confederate line abruptly collapsed. A few Texans held a bridge across Elk Creek long enough to save the Southern artillery, and Tandy Walker's Choctaw and Chickasaw with some Texas cavalrymen delayed the Union advance long enough for Cooper to draw off the main body of his army and their supply wagons.

The retreating Confederates fired all the buildings at Honey Springs as well as the supplies that had not been carried off, but Blunt's men managed to save large amounts of staples such as bacon, flour, sorghum, and salt.

The rotund little Kansan and his makeshift army thus brought an end to large-scale, massed Confederate military operations south of the Kansas border. After the victory at Honey Springs, the Confederates retreated south of the Canadian River in Indian Territory, followed by Colonel Judson's mounted brigade, while Blunt led the infantry east to Arkansas.

The Union successes east of the Mississippi and at Helena, Cabin Creek, and Honey Springs marked the turning point of the Civil War. The series of victories in these theaters cheered a dreadfully depressed Northern public. Southern sympathizers were incredulous at the series of defeats. But William Clarke Quantrill saw them as the windows of opportunity to strike back in his typically flamboyant way. He called his captains to a meeting in midsummer to outline his plan to wreak vengeance on an old and highly visible nest of Yankee abolitionism, Lawrence, Kansas.

It would be the greatest raid of the war and strike a blow at the symbol of all Northern things despised by Southerners. Perhaps it would catch the hated Kansas senator and general Jim Lane at home during the Congressional summer vacation, and above all, restore Quantrill's position as uncontested leader of the Confederate guerrilla forces.

The captains were lukewarm on the idea and dispersed without accepting Quantrill's plan. But then an accident occurred that brought them all together behind Quantrill.

Shortly after assuming command along the border, Gen. Thomas Ewing established a chain of military posts down the state line to slow the flow of bushwhackers entering Kansas. He also arrested and imprisoned the families of guerrillas in his district, and during the summer of 1863, large numbers of women and children were rounded up and jailed. They were confined in whatever buildings were available, some in disreputable condition.

One such facility was in a weakly constructed brick structure on Grand Avenue between 14th and 15th streets in Kansas City. The ground floor contained shops while the upper story, reached by an exterior stairway, was where the women were imprisoned. On August 13, 1863, it collapsed, killing five women and permanently crippling several more.

Among the casualties was a sister of William "Bloody Bill" Anderson, Cole Younger's cousin, and acquaintances of such notable guerrillas as George Todd, Frank and Jesse James, and William Gregg, leader of the best of the Border Ruffians. Maj. Preston Plumb of Emporia, Kansas, promptly surrounded the site of the tragedy with men armed with fixed bayonets, as rescuers searched the rubble for survivors and those who escaped screamed and wrung their hands with grief and disbelief.

Suddenly, Quantrill's plan looked appealing to all the irregulars. Their forces marshaled on August 16 in a camp along Missouri's Blackwater River. They set out the next morning for Kansas. They were joined that day by another 100 riders, led by a Col. D. Holt, and on August 20 another contingent of pistol-packing sympathizers joined up on the Grand River about five miles from the state line.

Late that afternoon, Quantrill's force of between 400 and 500 men rode into Kansas near Aubry, the much-abused community

*A large number of Missouri women were
rounded up and jailed.*

*The building collapsed, killing five women
and permanently crippling several more.*

a little south of Kansas City. They were observed by Kansas cav-alrymen at one of Ewing's posts who sent word north and south but failed to alert anyone west of their post.

The little garrison mustered, but their commander, Captain J.A. Pike, dared not attack or pursue because they were vastly outnumbered. The largest guerrilla force assembled during the war rode through much of the night to arrive on a low hill east of sleepy Lawrence at dawn on August 21.

Earlier in the month, the second largest city in Kansas had been alarmed by a report that Quantrill and his raiders were approaching, but when the attack failed to develop, vigilance was relaxed. When Quantrill really did come, he took the townspeople completely by surprise.

They rode past the outlying home of the Reverend Hugh Fisher, once a chaplain for the Lane Brigade. Fisher watched his neighbor, another pastor named S.J. Snyder, sit to milk his cow, only to be shot dead on his milking stool as a mob of marauders galloped by firing their numerous sidearms.

Fisher himself barely had time to conceal himself in his tiny cellar before the raiders came to his home seeking this known intimate of Jim Lane. Later in the morning, Fisher's wife lied more eloquently than might have been expected of a preacher's spouse to save him when the guerrillas returned.

The sun was barely up and roosters had just begun crowing when the hundreds of bushwhackers wearing hunting shirts, broad hats, and carrying four or more pistols apiece charged through the streets of Lawrence. Quantrill's orders were to"kill every man and burn every house." His cohorts scattered down the city streets, many carrying crude maps and lists of the names of Kansans Quantrill wanted killed.

A large column of the horsemen came upon the camp of twenty-two Union recruits, shooting them down to a man, tying their flag to a horse's tail, then riding on to the Lawrence hotels. At the Eldridge House, Kansas Provost Marshal Alexander Banks waved a white pillow case from a window and found he had surrendered the hotel's residents to Quantrill himself.

The bushwhacker leader sent the prisoners to a city hotel that was the headquarters of the raiders that morning. Then the guerrillas attacked the Johnson House, headquarters of the despised Yankee "Red Legs." There, many fleeing Union men were shot down.

Quantrill divided his men into street patrols to conduct house to house searches for men on the death lists and rob and burn the houses systematically. If a man answered the insistent pounding on the door of a house, he was shot down; if a woman replied, the marauders demanded money, watches, jewelry, even pieces of furniture.

The guerrillas felt that they were liberating considerable loot stolen previously from Missouri homes, and not without cause. Most women and children stood by helplessly, but a few wives rushed to the aid of their husbands only to be brushed aside or have their men shot in their arms. One man escaped hiding under a carpet as it was hauled out of his home. Jim Lane scampered away in his nightshirt to hide in a cornfield.

Quantrill gave explicit instructions that no woman was to be injured or accosted—and apparently none were. He also ordered that his headquarters hotel and its proprietor be spared. But after Quantrill had breakfasted and left, two bush-whackers who were looting and burning stores in the business district shot the surprised hotel owner and lit the place up. Quantrill's prisoners from the Eldridge House scattered out the back like a covey of quail. The pillaging and looting and killing orgy continued well past sunrise.

By 9 A.M., Quantrill decided to leave Lawrence, which was now engulfed in smoke and flame and populated by widows and orphans. Hundreds of tragic stories were left in their wake. With almost every guerrilla loaded with plunder, driving a remuda of a hundred loose horses and leading even more carrying dry goods from Lawrence stores, the by now thoroughly drunken column headed due south on the retreat to Missouri.

The bodies of scores of men dead or dying, white and black, littered the streets, boardwalks, alleys, porches, and yards. It has been estimated that there were between 150 and 200 dead, including a single guerrilla killed and two others wounded. More would never be found because their remains were burned in their own homes.

Upwards of a 1.5 million dollars in personal property was destroyed. It seemed that the irregulars had accomplished a Confederate coup in a summer of defeat, but like the rest of the vicious border war, retribution was terrible and the cycle began once more. Yet as Quantrill crossed the border to safety with all but one of his men, he basked in success.

Ewing's response to the sack of Lawrence—carried out right under the noses of his border outpost garrisons—was swift, decisive, and extreme. He issued the infamous Order No. 11 a mere four days after Lawrence burned. Already, thousands of

*Jim Lane scampered away in his
nightshirt to hide in a cornfield.*

Ruins of the Eldridge Hotel.

Union pursuers had followed Quantrill into Missouri to carry out their own orgy of burning, pillaging, and executions. This was an unexpected side effect Quantrill had not forseen, and Ewing chose to legitimize their dirty work.

Since his earlier attempts to protect his state of Kansas from the border ruffians had failed, he now decided that the only way to deny the guerrillas a safe haven was to depopulate the Missouri side of the state line. Order No. 11 expelled nearly 20,000 noncombatants from four counties, excepting only assigned areas near large towns such as county seats.

Throughout September, Kansas soldiers followed this order with a vengeance. They stole virtually everything portable and burned everything else. Order No. 11 specified that residents had to be gone in fifteen days, and by the first of October the Missouri counties next to Kansas were a desert dotted with the charred chimneys of civilian houses.

While the civilians were thus being punished, Federal troops fanned out searching for Quantrill. Of course, the bushwhackers had dispersed but up and down the line a brutal, gruesome kind of fighting now occurred as autumn approached. Kansas soldiers caught off guard by guerrillas were shot or hung; irregulars and more than a few innocent Missourians suffered the same fate when Kansans caught up with them. On October 4, 1863, one Kansas soldier wrote in his diary: "Quantrill has evidently gathered his bands and left, maybe for Kan., maybe for the South."

Probably basking in his notoriety, the bushwhacker leader was indeed headed south. As they had done in both 1861 and 1862, Quantrill and some of his strongest supporters took to the Texas Road to cross the Red River for the winter months. On the way south, Quantrill and several hundred guerrillas determined to strike yet another blow for the South following the Confederate victory at Chickamauga in September. Their target was on their way south—the Federal post at Baxter Springs.

Called Fort Blair and one of the posts established by Ewing

earlier in the year, the little cantonment consisted of some huts and some half-completed earthworks garrisoned by about a hundred white and African-American soldiers from a couple of Kansas regiments. Lt. James Pond and most of his small command had gathered on October 6 for a noonday meal when Quantrill and three hundred or four hundred riders charged across the prairie. The stolen blue uniforms worn by the guerrillas who rode over the partially finished earthworks fooled the Federal soldiers inside.

An unexpected added benefit came rolling down the road—General Blunt was moving his headquarters to Fort Smith with a wagon train, some reinforcements, and a band. When Quantrill rode toward Baxter Springs and the decimation of Lieutenant Pond's command, he saw Blunt's unsuspecting column.

The Rebels outnumbered both Federal outfits, so Quantrill formed some of his men company front. Blunt watched the blue-clad guerrillas lining up for battle, and he had not heard the shooting at the fort. Flattered to think little Fort Blair's garrison had turned out to greet the successful Kansas general, Blunt rode parallel to the column, planning a left face to salute the column opposite.

When the guerrillas opened fire with their sidearms, Blunt's escort scattered in panic. Blunt soon sat with an aid, Maj. H.Z. Curtis, son of Maj. Gen. Samuel R. Curtis, surrounded by between twenty and thirty dead or wounded Yankees. Assisting a woman accompanying his escort to mount an extra horse, they thus fled for their lives.

Curtis was killed by a flurry of shots that stuck his horse as well, and Blunt—never a comfortable horseman—made an ungainly escape. Mrs. Chester Thomas, wife of a Topekan traveling with Blunt, rode gracefully to safety.

Not so for the rest of the Union column. The band's wagon made a dash for the assumed safety of Fort Blair. A front wheel came off, spilling band members and instruments about the prairie where they were easy targets for mounted bushwhackers.

The unarmed musicians were brutally murdered as they attempted to dodge or seek safety, but there was none. Other guerrillas rode down and shot fleeing Yankees, killing or wounding two-thirds of Blunt's little command.

Inside the stockade, things were only slightly better. Pond rallied his black and white soldiers only after heroically and single-handedly firing the post's single small howitzer. Some of the Rebels had drawn off to participate in the attack on Blunt's wagon train. With sixty to eighty casualties among that command combined with the ease with which the guerrillas had sliced through the garrison causing more casualties, Quantrill seemed satisfied.

More dead and wounded, mostly African-Americans and a handful of Union Indians, were discovered around the fort, in the woods, and on the military road south. Quantrill finally called all his men together and gloated over another decisive victory, this one over the Yankee perceived by Southerners as the most successful Kansas general.

Quantrill led his guerrilla army out of Kansas for winter camp with Cooper's Texans and Confederate Indians. Thus, the bloodiest, most violent year of the war came to its conclusion. Quantrill felt as though he had salvaged what had turned out to be a disastrous year for the Confederacy. Few doubted that the following spring would bring the return of the guerrillas and renewed violence along the Kansas-Missouri border. It was a well-founded concern, but the next year would bring new challenges to Kansans.

CHAPTER 4

"Every Man . . . 18 to 60 to Arms": 1864-65

In the spring of 1864, Kansans again saw politics rise above most everything else in their minds. Although the war continued to be prosecuted on several fronts and most Kansas regiments were engaged, the elections scheduled for November of that year dominated many conversations. Naturally, speculation was rife about the renewal of the brutal border war, which promised to be even bloodier than it had been in 1863.

But Kansans would also begin to be troubled by another form of guerrilla warfare on its western frontier that had nothing to do with the Confederacy. An Indian war was brewing. And the optimism caused by victories in the summer of 1863 had been tempered by the terror of Quantrill's retaliatory raids, causing concern for the businesses, lives, and homes in every town in the state.

The attack on Lawrence gave Kansans pause. In the early fall of 1863, General Ewing sent word that Quantrill and a thousand of his men were 20 miles south of Independence, Missouri, preparing for an encore performance. All around the state—and now as far west as Topeka, Fort Riley, and Council Grove—public meetings were called to discuss various plans for defense. But in most cases all that was done was to alert the militia for possible service. Discussion was as far as most plans went for over a year, until the fall of 1864 brought renewed threats to eastern Kansas.

This was the leap year of the Civil War. Ladies in Topeka felt temporarily secure enough to use February 29, the additional day, as an excuse for a dance party. Amusements were few and far between, so the Episcopal ladies rented a stone hall and used boards as bleacher seating. The capital city was still a small town, and women were definitely a minority, so none of them could be wallflowers.

At this particular dance, a woman who was obviously expecting a child attended with her soldier husband. They danced until the husband tired, but while he rested and dozed by the warm stove, she refused to miss a single dance set. Late in the party she interrupted a dance set to search for her husband to go for the doctor. Their baby did not wait but was born about a half hour after the father left. It was one of the few parties the people of Topeka would witness during this stressful year.

Revivals were common among Kansas soldiers in the fourth spring of the war. During April, 1864, several regiments from the state experienced morale—and moral—improvement. In Leavenworth, in St. Louis, in Louisiana, Tennessee, and Georgia—perhaps in atonement for past sins, perhaps concerned about the consequences of future combat, maybe because as they grew older they confronted their own mortality—many among veteran Kansas regiments participated in religious revivals.

Some were conducted by the regimental chaplains. Others were itinerant tent shows catering to different outfits of large armies. Wrote one Kansas chaplain:

> . . . there is a decided improvement in the morals of the Reg. Quite a religious influence in Camp. At our prayer meeting 7 arose for prayer, with tears in their eyes told me that they resolved to lead new & Christian lives. There is every prospect of a revival. . . . I expect to draw one or two Hospital tents to-day for the purpose of having them to hold meetings in. . . . The Col. Appears willing to aid me in any thing I desire, to prosecute my work as Chap.

*Life in camp between actions was
often marked by boredom.*

During 1864, enlistments of many of the men in Kansas regiments expired. The 1st Kansas, after the Vicksburg campaign, was ordered back to Leavenworth to be mustered out. Two companies reenlisted. A vote of the 7th Kansas took place and, with a few exceptions, the regiment elected to reenlist, only a year after a company mutinied on account of whiskey.

By this vote, it was the only Kansas regiment to reenlist in a body, and it retained its organization and identity and was authorized to add the word "veteran" to its name. The men of the 7th Kansas Veteran Volunteer Cavalry were in a makeshift camp where they had been staying since New Year's Day. Without the benefit of tents, the men had gone into camp under a thick layer of snow, very rare in the state of Mississippi.

When the vote approached, representatives of the 7th Kansas tried to negotiate for the right to provide their cavalry mounts. The allowance of forty cents per day per man would have doubled each trooper's monthly pay. Gen. William T. Sherman, General Ewing's brother-in-law, ruled that the 7th had to reenlist unconditionally.

The regiments returned to the Kansas towns that most of their men called home or in which they were mustered in order to be demobilized or to be mustered in again. The 7th Kansas came home to Leavenworth, where several of the regiments had been recruited to a gala. The town was awake early, the Stars and Stripes flew from roof tops, and public buildings were decorated with red, white, and blue bunting.

The regiment that had been freebooters and slave-stealers at the outset of the war had redeemed itself in service in the Deep South. The troopers returned to Kansas vindicated, venerated as heroes. To celebrate their return, at 9 A.M. the 1st Kansas State Militia Regiment marched to the city limits to meet the veterans. The men of the 7th Kansas emerged from the gates of Fort Leavenworth and followed an honor guard. It was composed of Col. Charles R. Jennison, the first commander of the very regiment being honored, and some of his latest command, the 15th Kansas Volunteer Cavalry, a section of artillery, and a detachment of the Invalid Corps.

At the Leavenworth city limits, the militia fell in to lead the procession. Accompanied by the music of all three regimental bands, including that of the 7th Kansas, the parade wended its way through the city to the Turner Hall, where the returning regiment was greeted by its former lieutenant colonel, Daniel R. Anthony, now mayor of the city.

The 7th was at Fort Leavenworth in early February, but after its reenlistment went to St. Louis and then to Memphis to guard railroads. Elsewhere, the 11th, 15th, 16th, and 17th were stationed in Kansas during 1864. Two other Kansas regiments served in Tennessee. The 8th was given a rest after its ordeal at Chickamauga, but after recouping its strength at Leavenworth returned to Chattanooga. The 10th Kansas served on provost duty in Tennessee. The 2nd, 5th, part of the 6th, the 9th, 12th, 14th, and the 1st and 2nd Kansas Colored served in Arkansas.

On January 1, largely at the urging of Sen. Jim Lane, it was announced that President Lincoln had made Kansas a separate military department under the command of Gen. Samuel R. Curtis. The new department included Nebraska, Colorado Territory, and part of New Mexico Territory.

Despite a complaint on January 22, 1864, to Curtis that Kansas cavalry was raiding in the Central District of the Department of Missouri, the third year of the war started rather quietly. Brig. Gen. Egbert Brown, district commander, reported that the Kansans' forays into his district were robbing the remaining citizens of slaves and other property of every description.

Brown wrote in his report:

If Kansas wants negroes I will send 500 women and children to the State in two days, as they are a great annoyance to me, and everybody wants them removed. But they do not want them; they want the prosperity the negroes carry off and the opportunity of taking it by coming into the state.

For once, the 7th Kansas Cavalry was not among the Kansans crossing the border. That did not mean they were peaceful. They thoroughly enjoyed their furlough in Leavenworth. They also took the opportunity to fill gaps in their ranks. On February 19, 1864, 18-year-old William F. Cody got himself enlisted. He was a Pony Express rider at age 15, a member of an "independent company" that rustled horses and cattle from Missourians at 16, and a member of the Red Legs at 17. Several friends and Kansas neighbors had tried to convince him to join the regiment, but he avoided it.

"One day," wrote the future Buffalo Bill in his autobiography, "after having been under the influence of bad whiskey, I awoke to find myself a soldier in the 7th Kansas. I did not remember how or when I had enlisted."

Cody was mustered in on February 24 and assigned to Company H, 7th Kansas Veteran Volunteers. The rest of Cody's reminiscences as a Civil War soldier "become pure fantasy, tainted only slightly by reality."

Another serious Jayhawker who was not invading Missouri was James Montgomery. He led a regiment of African-Americans at the Battle of Olustee, Florida. Montgomery had been a Free-State leader in southern Kansas during the territorial years and an officer of Kansas troops early in the war. At the Battle of Olustee, or Ocean Pond, about 50 miles west of Jacksonville, three African-American regiments and six white regiments, supported by artillery and cavalry, were defeated by Confederates after a stubborn fight. Montgomery's regiment came into the fight at the very end, just in time to stop a Rebel charge and save the rest of the Federal force.

Maj. Gen. Samuel R. Curtis, first commander of the new District of Kansas, directed Brigadier General James Blunt to proceed to Fort Smith, Arkansas, to resume command of military operations in Indian Territory. Since December 1863, Col. William Phillips, with his Kansas Indian Brigade and white troops totaling about 1,500 cavalrymen, emulated Sherman's march through Georgia, punishing the members of the Five Civilized Tribes in the territory still in rebellion.

Before launching the scorched-earth campaign, Phillips told his followers: "Those who are still in arms are rebels, and ought to die. Do not kill a prisoner after he has surrendered. But I do not want you to take prisoners. I do ask you to make your footsteps severe and terrible."

Through the end of 1863 and the early part of 1864, Phillips' column marched about 400 miles, reported 250 Confederates killed, and returned to Fort Gibson without losing a single man. General Blunt arrived in Arkansas to take command under the order establishing the Department of Kansas which specified that the department included the "military post of Fort Smith." When Blunt arrived he was incensed to learn that the order had been interpreted literally, and the town of Fort Smith was under control of Brig. Gen. John M. Thayer of the Department of Arkansas.

All Blunt commanded was the military post, a "stone enclosure about 200 feet square." Most of the troops in the area were billeted in the town. Blunt tried controlling all Union troops by withholding rations unless they reported to him, but complaints and demands for his removal rose all the way to Gen. Ulysses S. Grant. Grant directed Curtis to remove Blunt from command at Fort Smith, so Curtis then assigned the Kansas general to a small area in western Kansas with only 300 troops at his disposal.

Blunt was not the only problem officer for Curtis. General Ewing and his infamous Order No. 11 had become an embarrassment. On February 28, 1864, Curtis got him away from the border, too, assigning him to command Colorado Territory. Although Ewing would use the influence of his brother-in-law, General Sherman, to move from this out-of-the-way theater to St. Louis, there was need for a military presence in the area to which Blunt and Ewing were sent.

Several parties of Indian raiders attacked wagon trains on the Santa Fe Trail west of Fort Larned. Other raiders stole livestock from settlers in eastern Colorado. During the investigation by members of the garrison of one of the latter incidents, it was learned that a family of four white settlers had been brutally killed by Plains Indian warriors thought to be Cheyenne. Their identity would later be challenged, but the Cheyenne were still blamed.

The blame led to gruesome results late in the year when the village of Cheyenne leader Black Kettle and the lodges of Arapaho chieftain White Antelope were attacked by ninety-day Colorado volunteers. Scores of Indians were massacred at Sand Creek by the merciless 3rd Colorado Volunteer Cavalry from Denver under Col. John Chivington. Women, children, and the elderly fell victim to the white soldiers, and some atrocities were committed.

Some Unionist newspaper editors accused Confederates of stirring up the wild Indians on the frontier, but it was really a clash of cultures and poor treatment by Federal officials and civilians that caused the Indian war. Before the Civil War, Fort Larned was garrisoned by companies of the 2nd U.S. Infantry augmented by companies of the 2nd U.S. Dragoons. With the war in progress, the regular army units were transferred to the east and the post was occupied by companies of volunteers from Kansas, Colorado Territory, and Wisconsin. These units changed from time to time, but for the most part the garrison consisted of Lt. W.E. Crocker's 9th Wisconsin Battery, Light Artillery.

As spring rolled around, Kansas regiments became active in several theaters of the war. The 8th returned to Leavenworth, where it had been recruited, but in April it returned to Chattanooga. It joined the drive to Atlanta and took a small part in the Battle of Nashville. The 10th Kansas served on provost duty, and its members who were not mustered out in the summer were sent to Tennessee as well.

Arkansas was a state in which many Kansans served. The 2nd Kansas was ordered to join Gen. Frederick Steele in a campaign to capture Camden. Some companies of the 6th were there while others in Colonel Judson's regiment were attached to Colonel Phillips's Union Indian Brigade and scouted along the Arkansas River. The 9th Kansas was also attached to Steele's army, but the general advanced on Camden without waiting for another division of Kansas regiments.

On April 11, the Union army fought the Battle of Prairie D'Ane against Missouri Confederates under generals Shelby, Marmaduke, and Price. Camden fell on April 16, but because Gen. Nathaniel Banks had failed to achieve his objective further south on the Red River, Steele had to fall back.

Although Banks did not engulf and destroy Kirby-Smith's smaller Confederate army, his expedition did draw Confederates away from the southern Kansas border to focus on the threat in Louisiana.

On April 18, 1864, the 1st Kansas Colored Infantry—heroes of Cabin Creek and Honey Springs—was decimated in one of the most infamous battles of the American Civil War. A Federal supply train of about 200 wagons filled with forage for Yankee cavalry with Steele was surprised at Poison Springs, Arkansas. The Union force guarding the wagon train was heavily outnumbered by the Rebel attackers, consisting of Texans of Col. Richard Gano's brigade and Col. Tandy Walker's Confederate 2nd Indian Brigade.

The Federal escort included the African-American soldiers of the 1st Kansas Colored Infantry. Perhaps some of Gano's Texans had been among those who had been ignominiously defeated at the hands of the African-Americans, or perhaps they were adhering to an order issued by Kirby-Smith that all black soldiers and their white officers should receive no quarter.

Whatever the reason, the Texans fell on the men of the 1st Kansas Colored with no mercy. African American soldiers who attempted to surrender, even knowing they risked being returned to slavery, were shot to death. The 1st Kansas Colored Volunteer regiment was nearly annihilated in a massacre of black soldiers second only to that at Fort Pillow, Tennessee, as devastated as the 54th Masssachusetts in front of Charleston, South Carolina.

After the atrocity, "Remember Poison Springs!" became a battle cry as poignant as "Remember the Alamo." Survivors of the decimated 1st Kansas Colored and their colleagues in the 2nd Kansas Colored Infantry, along with their white officers, would no longer take prisoners. Instead, they would serve up some of the same cold steel that had killed their comrades.

Such a view only made the vicious border war even more ugly and desperate, if that was possible. After Poison Springs, every clash between the two African-American regiments from Kansas and any Rebels became virtually a fight to the death, with no quarter asked or given by either side.

It seemed that the border war was about to heat up again, too. Three days later, on April 21, when the Kansas Republicans met in Topeka to select delegates to their party's national convention in Baltimore, Colonel Phillips wired General Curtis in Leavenworth. Quantrill and the guerrillas who still acknowledged him as leader were on the move. They had slipped through Federal lines past the patrols of the 6th Kansas Cavalry and crossed the Arkansas River on the night of April 20.

Farther east, other Southern partisans in southwest Arkansas realized that most Federal troops had been withdrawn from the Fort Smith area to participate in Steele's Camden campaign. Outbreaks of guerrilla fighting occurred throughout the month of April. A few companies of the 2nd Kansas and the 6th Kansas Cavalry regiments were all that remained on the south side of the Arkansas River.

During early April, concerted attacks had been made by irregulars in large numbers. A particularly stiff fight was conducted by two companies of the 2nd and a company of the 6th that were attacked at Roseville, Arkansas, by about 500 partisans. Some of the Rebels donned blue uniforms and committed depredations in the vicinity of the old Prairie Grove battlefield while pretending to be members of the 14th Kansas Cavalry.

At the end of April, General Steele's division was falling back from its campaign against Camden. Col. William F. Cloud of the 2nd Kansas Cavalry commanded Steele's cavalry brigade, which was charged with the division's rear guard. At 2 P.M. on April 29, the Federal column arrived at Jenkin's Ferry on the Saline River. There was a steady downpour of rain all afternoon. A pontoon bridge across the Saline allowed Union forces to start crossing the swollen stream, but not before the Confederates of Gen. Sterling Price's army attacked the Federal rear.

Two companies of the 6th Kansas Cavalry served as a picket to cover the crossing of troops and supply wagons on the pontoon bridge. The demonstrations against the Union rear on April 29 were harbingers of an attack in force against the Federals falling back through central Arkansas. The rain fell during much of the night.

The Battle of Jenkin's Ferry on April 30, 1864, involved several Kansas units. The 2nd Kansas Colored Infantry, now commanded by Col. Samuel J. Crawford, and the 12th Kansas Infantry, led by Lt. Col. J.E. Hayes, defended the left flank of the Union army, helping drive a Rebel attack off the field. Later in the day, the two regiments were split and joined units from Illinois, Indiana, Iowa, and Wisconsin.

Another Rebel attack was fended off as the infantry protected the pontoon bridge and the remaining wagons of the Yankee supply train. The 2nd and 12th Kansas had already crossed the pontoons over the Saline.

At one point late in the morning after a rebel drive was repulsed, Colonel Crawford requested permission for his 2nd Kansas Colored to charge a Rebel battery. With fixed bayonets, the regiment captured the battery, removing the guns from the field with ropes. At the same time the 12th Kansas Infantry took part in a nasty firefight on the Federal left. One last attack on the left was repulsed by the 12th Kansas and some Iowa companies, and the battle ended by half past noon. By 2 P.M. the last of the Yankees were across the river, the pontoon bridge was destroyed behind them, and the battle was over.

During the summer of 1864, Kansans on the home front found themselves lulled into a false sense of security. Much of the anticipated renewal of guerrilla warfare failed to materialize. Quantrill's star waned as other, lesser guerrilla captains such as Bloody Bill Anderson siphoned off manpower. Rather than raiding Kansas towns, many of the captains now sought vengeance against Missouri Unionists and any Federal soldiers on whom they could lay their hands.

With the exception of a few small incidents, the guerrilla war shifted east to Missouri. Kansas regiments outside the state settled into provost, patrol, and escort duties. Some, like the 5th Kansas, saw most of their men discharged by the end of 1864.

Although early in the summer citizens of most of the larger towns met to discuss protection plans for their cities, discussion was as far as the plans went for much of the summer. A new threat on the western Kansas frontier drew military attention.

There had been violent clashes along the Smoky Hill and Santa Fe Trails as the Cheyenne and Arapaho increased the ferocity of their resistance. Along these routes new forts were established for military protection of travelers and settlers. A company of Iowa cavalry commanded by a young lieutenant named Ellsworth founded Fort Ellsworth on the Smoky Hill River about 60 miles west of Fort Riley.

Fort Zarah was created on the Great Bend of the Arkansas River to protect the Santa Fe Trail. Fort Zarah was named after the son of General Curtis, who had been with General Blunt's small force and died in the fighting at Baxter Springs. Companies of regiments from Wisconsin, Iowa, and Colorado Territory, as well as elements of the 11th Kansas Cavalry, were assigned to these posts and patrolled vast areas of the high plains tracking down alleged red raiders.

At the same time Gen. Robert B. Mitchell, hero commander of the 2nd Kansas at Wilson's Creek, was sent to end the Indian war in Nebraska Territory, especially along the Platte River Road, providing protection for stage coaches and freighters trains bound for Denver and Salt Lake. Mitchell had at his disposal elements of several Iowa cavalry regiments, including an officer who had also been at Wilson's Creek in an Iowa regiment and who would settle in Fort Scott after the war, Eugene F. Ware.

Also that summer, gold in Montana and Idaho Territories drew a new flood of fortune seekers, some of them deserters from both Union and Confederate armies, further aggravating the Plains Indians.

As summer turned to autumn, a last gasp of the Confederacy caused renewed concern among the citizens of Kansas. Gen. Sterling Price led two divisions of Missourians and a division under Arkansas Brig. Gen. James Fagan in an invasion of Missouri. Price was allegedly the "military commander" of the shadowy Order of American Knights, and he coordinated his invasion with guerrilla attacks behind Union lines as well as encouraging the loosely organized irregular units to join his troops. His original objective was probably St. Louis, but finding Union defenses stouter than he anticipated in the eastern half of Missouri, he turned west.

During the time that Price's Rebel army was on the state border, the question of defense once again rose in towns throughout Kansas. It was considered necessary to take precautions to protect almost every town and village on the border, as in the young capital city, "should any stragglers from Price's command come this way."

Topeka was an example. A force of woodcutters gathered elm and cottonwood logs from along the Kansas River for a stockade. The logs were set in the ground about three feet deep in a circle with the bark side out. Loopholes were cut in each log—one for firing while standing and one for the kneeling position—and four openings were left for small cannon.

The stockade was dubbed "Fort Simple," and all men not at the front were engaged in digging rifle pits in which sharpshooters could lie in relative safety. Reports of guerrillas and Rebel stragglers were rife throughout the state, and at least once the residents of Topeka were so convinced of an impending attack—probably by Quantrill, everyone assumed—that they buried their treasures and manned the trenches.

Among those standing guard at Fort Simple one night were three women masquerading as men. Only dawn revealed their true gender.

As Price's invaders moved into Missouri, the secessionists met their first setback at Pilot Knob. A force of about 1,000 Federals commanded by none other than Gen. Thomas Ewing, Jr., author of the infamous Order No. 11 the year before, held a hastily constructed fort against assaults by 7,000 Confederates. Casualties were lopsided—1,500 Confederates versus 200 Union men.

Price headed toward Jefferson City after determining that St. Louis was too well protected for his forces to subdue. So was the Missouri capital city. Recruits and guerrilla bands, including Bloody Bill Anderson, joined Price as he turned west toward Kansas.

When it became known that Price was heading toward Kansas, General Curtis hastily summoned his available troops. Some of his men were with Blunt chasing Indians on the frontier. Curtis urged Gov. Thomas Carney to call out the state militia to supplement the 11th, 14th, 15th, 16th, and 17th Kansas regiments and the 2nd Kansas Artillery battery.

Estimates of Price's force ranged from 5,000 to 30,000, but in fact with recruits and irregulars the Confederate army probably numbered only about 12,000 men. Nevertheless, this threat was enough to convince Governor Carney to follow the advice of Curtis, and on October 8 he activated the militia.

1864 was an election year. Voters in Kansas would vote in the national election, chosing between incumbent President Abraham Lincoln and Democratic Party candidate Gen. George B. McClellan, former commander of the eastern Army of the Potomac. It was also an election year in Kansas and cutthroat political competition occurred between U.S. Sen. Jim Lane and Gov. Thomas Carney.

The governor was busy with the last month of his campaign against Lane's hand-picked candidate, Samuel J. Crawford of the 2nd Kansas Colored Infantry. Crawford took advantage of his notoriety for leading his African-American troops at the battles of Prairie D'Ane and Jenkin's Ferry earlier in the year, and Lane used his political savvy and chicanery against Carney and the moderate Republicans.

The military crisis came at a time when it seemed that Carney had finally found the key to defeating Jim Lane's demagoguery and the Radical Republican Party was in decline. It appeared that the majority of voters backed Carney and the moderates. Lincoln might even be defeated in Kansas the next month.

The political campaign was interrupted by the flood of news, the military campaign, and Price's raid, not to mention the call for militia aid from Curtis. The general hoped to move both militia and volunteers east into Missouri to meet Price in the hilly country beyond Kansas City, where the Rebel cavalry would be least effective, but he was stymied by the opposition to crossing the state line that the militiamen put forth.

Governor Carney pointed out that state law provided for the militia to defend Kansas. His moderate faction of the Republican Party wished to have no state militia serve outside Kansas. If they were inside the state on election day, they could vote in the state election, but if they were in Missouri they could not—and Lane's chances of success would be vastly improved.

Not above stooping to the tactics of Lane's partisan politicians, Carney supporters went so far as to circulate newspapers and broadsides which declared that Price was no longer even in Missouri. The political situation in Kansas flared again, and the campaign against the Rebels was called "an egregious humbug."

Foiled in his attempts at St. Louis and Jefferson City, Price now focused his attention on Leavenworth. He hoped to capture the large Federal supply depot at Fort Leavenworth as well as reduce the nest of hated abolitionists and breeding ground for radical Kansans fond of marauding in Missouri. Following the Missouri River valley, Price had arrived at Harrison, Missouri, about the time Curtis gathered his men, recalled General Blunt from the plains to command a division of volunteers, and called for the militia.

Two days after the militia was called out, General Curtis proclaimed martial law throughout the Department of Kansas and ordered every man between the ages of 18 and 60 years, white or black, to arms and to the border. About 12,000 men in some fifteen regiments responded to the call. The Union army in front of Price was divided into two divisions—the volunteer division commanded by Blunt and consisting mainly of the five Kansas volunteer regiments, and the militia division under Brig. Gen. George W. Deitzler.

About 12,000 militiamen in fifteen regiments
responded and marched to the border.

General Deitzler had begun his career as a Kansas soldier as colonel of the famous 1st Kansas Volunteer Infantry at Wilson's Creek. He had risen to become adjutant general of the Kansas State Militia and now commanded the militia division of the Army of the Border.

Each unit of the militia had to provide its own supplies and transportation. Individuals each provided "two blankets, a tin cup, knife and fork, and a haversack." In addition, some of the men in militia regiments were issued new Enfield rifles from Fort Leavenworth in place of old and virtually useless carbines that had been distributed immediately after Quantrill's raid on Lawrence.

Portions of Blunt's division engaged Price's Confederates on October 18 near Lexington, Missouri. Price had fought a successful battle at Lexington two years before, defeating a smaller but well-forted up Federal force by advancing his Rebel troops behind the portable protection of rolling bales of hemp. Now, Blunt's Yankees faced the same foe. Again, superior numbers made them fall back. The rest of Curtis's force, now designated the Army of the Border, advanced along parallel roads to the line of the Big Blue River just east and south of Kansas City.

Curtis turned out civilians in Kansas City to the Big Blue banks to assist soldiers fortifying the stream. The civilians consisted mainly of Irish, German, and black men who were from Kansas City, Missouri, so not subject to the call-up of militia in Kansas. At the main fords of the Big Blue, they felled trees, made abattis, and built barricades.

By this time, Curtis had learned that a full division of cavalry called the Provisional Cavalry Division, commanded by legendary Yankee horse soldier Maj. Gen. Alfred Pleasonton, was in hot pursuit of Price. He was followed only slightly more slowly by a division of volunteer infantry led by Maj. Gen. A.J. Smith. Blunt's division lay between Price and Leavenworth, but if Price could be held at the border before crossing into Kansas his invasion could be stymied and perhaps his army destroyed.

On October 19, 1864, Blunt met Price's lead elements under the inimitable Jo Shelby, now a general and leader of his Missouri Iron Brigade—the best Confederate cavalry outfit in the Trans-Mississippi West—at Lexington. Blunt knew that he had to hold the Rebels as long as he could to give Curtis time to finish the defensive line of the Big Blue and to allow Pleasonton time to catch up.

Blunt conferred with his aides, Col. John T. Burris and Sen. Jim Lane, who took time from his busy political campaign to participate in the urgent military campaign, to plan a series of delays. While his division prepared to withdraw toward Independence, Missouri, Blunt ordered the best of his regiments, the 11th Kansas Cavalry under Col. Thomas Moonlight, and four mountain howitzers to cover the retreat.

Moonlight was an adventurous man who led a colorful career as a Kansas soldier. At 13, he ran away from his home in Scotland and worked his way across the Atlantic Ocean to America. As a child, he worked at odd jobs until he was old enough to enlist in the army. Moonlight served in the U.S. Army until 1858, when he retired to be a gentleman farmer near Leavenworth.

The War Between the States brought the fiery little Scot back into the service. He raised a battery of Union artillery, and during the next three years rose to the rank of colonel. He would gain fame for leading a brigade including his own regiment—the 11th Kansas Cavalry—in the series of delaying actions that allowed Curtis, Blunt, and other Union officers to organize the defense of Kansas City against Price's invading Confederates.

Moonlight's regiment made four stands within six miles, holding off the Rebel advance until darkness on Wednesday, October 19. The Southerners bivouacked in the field while Blunt marched until 2 A.M. to the Little Blue River east of Independence, Missouri.

At the Little Blue, Blunt urged Curtis to advance, join forces with him, and make a major stand. Curtis refused to leave the line of the Big Blue and ordered Blunt to fall back to Independence, leaving Colonel Moonlight and his belea- guered 11th Kansas to guard the crossing of the Little Blue.

Moonlight spent all day October 20 preparing his meager force. His howitzers were placed to cover the only bridge, but the river was so shallow that it could be crossed at any point. However, the banks were steep and heavily timbered, so Moonlight formed his regiment into a line of heavy pickets. Throughout the autumn afternoon, Moonlight's troopers waited, but no Rebels showed themselves.

Dawn on Friday, October 21, brought a flurry of activity in the Confederate camp. While General Blunt organized rein- forcements to relieve Moonlight, Rebel Gen. John S. Marmaduke's cavalrymen attacked the Kansans along the Little Blue in force. The first company of Marmaduke's divi- sion fell upon Moonlight's pickets a mile east of the river. The pickets fell back under pressure until they reached Moonlight's line. The Confederates charged, hoping to seize the bridge. A third of the Rebels in the attack went down in the initial firing. Moonlight's 11th Kansas doggedly defended the Little Blue. At times, the contest was hand-to-hand as the Rebels charged with revolvers and sabers.

Blunt hurried his relief force of 1,900 men of the 2nd Colorado Volunteer Cavalry and the Colorado Battery supple- mented by the 4th, 12th, and 19th Kansas State Militia regi- ments to Moonlight's aid. With Col. James Ford of the 2nd Colorado as brigade commander, Blunt enjoyed some early success repulsing the Rebel advance. Then Curtis arrived on the scene and countermanded Blunt's orders.

Ford and his men had little choice but to follow Curtis's instructions, but although Blunt thought Curtis confused his men, they showed little sign of being mixed up. Even though the reinforcements brought the number of Union defenders to 2,500, it was obvious the bluecoats could not hold out for long, especially when Jo Shelby's division joined Marmaduke's men. The bridge across the Little Blue was fired.

The Union troops fell back slowly, in good order, fighting all the way. The fight at the Little Blue, the first day of the three-day Battle of Westport, was a long, drawn-out affair, eight hours altogether. Blunt made an effort to get 10,000 militiamen into position to counter Confederate attacks but with little success because of a conflict of command—General Deitzler refused to allow Blunt to assume authority over any more of his militia division.

So Blunt's force made a stand wherever possible, retreated whenever too hard pressed. Blunt, Ford, and Moonlight retreated west through Independence, where violent street fighting took place and thereby gained Curtis one more day to prepare the line of the Big Blue River. It also brought Pleasonton's cavalry division to just a day's ride from the Rebel rear.

That night Daniel Boutwell, a volunteer from Topeka, made a daring journey to carry the plans Curtis had made to Pleasonton. Taking a skiff on the Missouri River at about 7 P.M., Boutwell tried to skirt the north flank of the Rebel army. But the skiff sank, so he had to swim to shore, then creep through thickets and ravines past Southern pickets, some of whom spotted and fired on him. He found himself sinking in quicksand before he reported to Pleasonton that Curtis was prepared to withstand Price on the Big Blue and urged the cavalry to all speed.

Curtis believed the Rebels would make their drive along the Kansas City-to-Independence road against his strong fortifications at the main ford of the Big Blue. Blunt argued that the Confederates would only feint at the breastworks and abattis, then flank the Union right at one of the other fords. Acting without approval from Curtis, Blunt sent a brigade under the old Jayhawker, Charles R. Jennison, to Byram's Ford, five miles south of the main crossing. Colonel Jennison's men filled the ford with felled timber and lined the country lane with abattis.

As Blunt had predicted, on Saturday, October 22, Price's troops demonstrated on the Federal left and center but struck decisively on the Union right flank. Severe fighting took place at Byram's Ford and on a farm called the Mockabee place. Gen. Jo Shelby's secessionist division crossed the Big Blue under Jennison's guns early that afternoon. Col. Sidney Jackman dismounted part of his brigade to attempt a frontal assault, but by 2 P.M. Shelby concluded the ford could not be forced. He sent Col. Frank B. Gordon with the 5th Missouri Confederate Cavalry upstream and Lt. Col. Alonzo Slayback with his Missouri Confederate Cavalry Battalion downstream to search for a crossing. Neither went far before discovering possible fords.

General Curtis quickly became alarmed at the halfhearted efforts of Confederate Colonel Jackman's pressure on the main crossing of the Big Blue. Only then did Curtis realize that the Rebel attack against his fortified line would come at some crossing other than the ford where he laid such elaborate plans. He frantically dispatched a message to his Union subordinate, Gen. M.S. Grant—no relation to the famous Gen. Ulysses S. Grant—whose headquarters was at Hickman Mills, to look out for his position.

He issued orders to send scouts out to see if Price was moving on the right flank and report back every thirty minutes. The mounted portion of the 2nd Kansas State Militia Regiment from Topeka and the county around it under Col. George W. Veale became one of Grant's scouting parties. Colonel Veale and the mounted battalion of his regiment rode out on reconnaissance but saw nothing of the enemy.

Shelby's division finally forced a crossing of Byram's Ford at about 3 P.M. Slayback and Gordon flanked Jennison's bluecoats of the 15th Kansas Cavalry on both sides, and the Federal troops fell back to Westport in order to avoid encirclement. Several Rebel regiments forded the river near Hickman Mills, reached the crest of a ridge, and wheeled north, flanking Curtis's line of defense. Jackman's dismounted men then charged across Byram's Ford so fast that the Yankee axes used to fell trees were left behind.

Shelby and Fagan poured their Southern divisions through the break in the Yankee line. Jennison and his ragtag force of cavalry and militia regrouped after the attack and held together long enough to withdraw a battery of field pieces, then fell back steadily. The Rebels pushed Curtis's right flank northward across a stream known as Brush Creek into the town of Westport.

Rebel Colonel Gordon and his 5th Missouri Confederate Cavalry crossed the Big Blue near Hickman Mills and found themselves squarely between two Union forces—Jennison's, which was collapsing at Byram's Ford, and General Grant's militia at Hickman Mills. Upon receiving Curtis's warning that Price would attempt a river crossing on the right of the Union line, Grant immediately sent large reconnoitering parties in all directions, scattering his command. Gordon's regiment might have been crushed, but Grant was in no position to aid Jennison when the breakthrough occurred at Byram's Ford.

The day was fading when that raw regiment of Kansas militia from Topeka and Shawnee County made a stand that helped determine the outcome of the battle. The fight of the 2nd Kansas State Militia at the Mockabee farm was short but fierce and decisive. General Grant made his stand, forming his line alongside a howitzer known as the Topeka Battery under Captain Ross Burns that was part of the 2nd K.S.M. in the road bordering the farm. Like seasoned veterans, the Kansas farmers held their position and returned rebel fire. With their line finally broken in some confusion, the militiamen hastily reformed and returned to their deadly task.

Heavy rifle and howitzer fire repulsed the first Confederate charge. Colonel Jackman ordered Colonel Gordon's regiment back in another attempt, but this one was repulsed in less time than the first. Shelby was getting desperate to force the road open, complete the flanking movement, and prepare to drive into Kansas. Colonel Jackman arranged his full brigade for a final, overwhelming charge.

One Rebel yell, then Jackman's full brigade charged upon

The fight at the Mockabee farm was short but fierce.

some 500 Kansas militiamen. For a few moments, the battle raged fiercely around a stone wall on the Mockabee farm, the narrow lane, and especially around the single howitzer of the Topeka Battery blocking the road. However, the superior numbers of veteran Rebel cavalrymen finally crushed the Topeka and Shawnee County militiamen. Of the 500 untrained Kansas citizens, 24 died, 24 were wounded, and 68 were captured.

The pent-up hatreds of the border war and frustration at the stiff Yankee resistance caused tempers to flare. Several of the prisoners were fired upon and wounded, and several died later of these wounds. At least one African-American with the 2nd K.S.M. had his throat cut, obviously not a battle wound. More probably suffered the same fate.

The wounded were cared for during the night of October 22 and all day on Sunday, October 23, behind Union lines in

The wounded were cared for during the night of October 22.

Kansas City. But the bold stand of the battalion stopped Jackman's Confederate brigade from marching into Kansas, turning the southern flank of the Army of the Border.

At sundown on October 22, General Pleasonton sent a message from Independence saying that he was pursuing Price with 20,000 men. After Pleasonton received Pvt. Daniel Boutwell's information that Curtis was ready for combat, the cavalry commander moved swiftly. Pleasonton hastily constructed a makeshift bridge over the Little Blue River, replacing the original structure that Colonel Moonlight had burned the previous day.

He then crossed his troops, train, and artillery, maintaining close contact with the Rebels all day on October 22. He fought the Rebels at Independence on the field of Moonlight's fight the day before. The Yankees drove Marmaduke's division through the streets of Independence in a hand-to-hand struggle.

On the opposite side of the Southern army, General Blunt had formed a new line of defense running east and west, facing the Rebels to the south, just north of the town of Westport. The 2nd Kansas State Militia Regiment had given the brigadier time to reform his troops by withstanding Shelby's onslaught earlier that day. General Curtis was shaken by the failure of his Army of the Border to hold the line along the Big Blue River and was pessimistic about the chances for his army when fighting was rejoined the next morning.

Not even a reassuring message from Pleasonton and the booming thunder of the latter's cannon beyond the Rebel army lifted Curtis' spirits. Had it not been for the more energetic and imaginative Blunt, the Army of the Border might have withdrawn into the defenses of Kansas City that night.

The Confederates were no less anxious in their camp on top of the hills around Kansas City and Westport. Shelby sent an officer to Price to suggest a night withdrawal to save the army. He received no reply.

The night was bitterly cold, below freezing, the air thick and hazy until a chill wind began blowing. The Rebel troopers huddled under skimpy blankets behind their hurriedly constructed breastworks atop the hill. Not a few of them were aware of their predicament, but they had supreme confidence in the experience and skill of their generals. Most of them knew that Shelby and Marmaduke had escaped from bad spots before and were sure that they could do so again.

The fighting on October 23—a clear, cold Sunday morning—began with the desultory firing of small arms, but it rapidly became a major artillery duel. The two Yankee armies on either side of Price's Confederates pushed toward one another, effectively squeezing the Southerners to the east. The Union infantry force under A.J. Smith joined Pleasonton's cavalry, and the combined forces tried to cut off the Rebels from the east and close the trap in which the Confederates found themselves. Price ordered Shelby and Fagan to turn eastward, support Marmaduke's withdrawal from Pleasonton's attack, and then concentrate around the wagon train.

The Confederates then started the 500 wagons and their prisoners south with the intention of striking the military road to Fort Scott, in southeastern Kansas. The entire procession was guarded by several thousand troops.

Rain began falling shortly after the Rebel army turned southward on the afternoon of October 23. The roads became slippery with mud, but the continued presence of Federal pursuit spurred the Confederates in their efforts to escape. It would have been hard enough to slog along at a normal pace under such conditions. The steady, icy rain turned the unpaved roads into bottomless quagmires and left the marchers to struggle to keep from becoming completely bogged down.

But the Rebel army had to hurry to stay ahead of their Union pursuers, who pressed to maintain close contact with them. The mounted Southerners made their prisoners run along through the ankle-deep sludge as the Rebels managed to pull themselves, their wagons, and their artillery out of the mire and went slogging on down the road.

Price finally achieved one of the goals that he had set for himself on that rainy, dreary Sunday—he crossed the border into Kansas. But he had fallen short of total success, for he was headed south, in the opposite direction from Fort Leavenworth. His weary army marched all night on the military road from Fort Leavenworth to Fort Scott. Throughout the night of October 23 and all during the day of October 24, it made its way through a nasty drizzle. At last it stopped long after dark on Monday night near the Marais des Cygnes River, utterly dispirited.

All were dispirited, that is, except the ever-optimistic Price. He felt confident that by this time he had saved his army. He was so confident, in fact, that he laid plans the night of October 24 for Shelby to range ahead of the main body of the army with a part of his division on the following morning to raid Fort Scott and capture even more military supplies.

Shelby never reached Fort Scott. He was well on his way the afternoon of Tuesday, October 25, when he received an urgent summons from Price reporting an imminent attack by Pleasonton's Provisional Cavalry Division near a stream called Mine Creek. A running fight of several miles ensued while Shelby dashed back to Price's army. To save the wagon train, Marmaduke and Fagan formed a line of battle to hold the Northern cavalry at bay.

With little preparation, two of Pleasonton's brigades were ordered to charge across the prairie at a gallop while the Confederates hastened to cross Mine Creek in Linn County, Kansas, a short distance south of the Marais des Cygnes River. Half a dozen mounted regiments massed on the road to Fort Scott, intent on sweeping over the Rebels through sheer strength of numbers. In columns of regiments, the Federal cavalrymen charged forward, expecting to destroy Price's army in one fell swoop.

But Marmaduke, whose Rebel division formed the first line of defense for the Confederate army, ordered a counter-charge. The blue and butternut lines clashed at full speed. In

Pleasonton's brigades charged across the prairie at a gallop while the Confederates hastened to cross Mine Creek.

a matter of minutes, the Yankee horse soldiers captured Marmaduke, another Rebel general, four colonels, a thousand enlisted men, and ten pieces of artillery. Only the timely arrival of Shelby and his Iron Brigade prevented the capture of the train and utter destruction of the Confederate army. With about 25,000 men from both sides involved, the Battle of Mine Creek was the largest engagement fought on Kansas soil during the war.

The Union prisoners had had no food and little water since their capture several days earlier. One recalled that "in crossing a stream, which of course was stirred up by the hurrying army, we would catch up a little in our hats or in tins and drink as we ran." Shortly after the Mine Creek fight, A.J. Huntoon, a captain of the 2nd Kansas State Militia Regiment, sought some relief for the prisoners' situation by convincing some guards to take him to the Confederate headquarters. But when they arrived at the cluster of tents and wagons, there was no one there.

Personal belongings and clothing such as overcoats and shoes were taken from the prisoners, and in the freezing weather the captives were forced to cover themselves with worn-out blankets. Their Rebel captors had eaten no better. General Shelby once rode alongside the captured Yankees and told them, "Gentlemen, I am doing the best I can; you are getting just as good fare as my men are."

Shelby frequently rode back to the prisoners, always with a cheerful word for them, attempting to reassure them. He was one of the few Confederates for whom the Kansans held any respect, albeit grudging respect.

Price's fighting retreat continued from daybreak far into darkness each day after Mine Creek, with Pleasonton's volunteers pressing him every step of the way. The column left the Mine Creek battlefield at 2 A.M. on the morning of October 26. There was no hope of rest for either the Rebels or their unfortunate Yankee prisoners.

Always there was constant marching. The prisoners and dismounted rebels tramped on interminably on rubbery legs, barely able to stand. Forced marches of such duration were telling on hardened soldiers under the best of conditions. The crude, crooked, unpaved, rain-soaked roads of Kansas were difficult to traverse for the captured militiamen of the 2nd Kansas State Militia Regiment.

One of the Union prisoners, Samuel J. Reader, at one point felt that he could go no farther, so he grasped desperately at the tail of one of the preceding guard's horse and was literally dragged on his feet. Some of those on foot were forced to cut their shoes from their feet because of the severe swelling and to return circulation by vigorous rubbing before they lost their feet.

The Rebel forces were in precipitous retreat. Union cavalry-men again struck the Confederate rear guard near the Little Osage River back in Missouri. By Wednesday afternoon, near Carthage, Missouri, seven prisoners and one Rebel soldier were so exhausted that they were left at a vacant farm house a couple miles south of the town. When the Rebel was discovered by Colonel Jennison's 15th Kansas Volunteers, he was promptly hanged from an apple tree.

A week after the Battle of Westport the fatigued Southern column marched into Newtonia, in the southwest corner of Missouri. The Confederates had traversed nearly the entire length of the Kansas-Missouri border in their retreat, harassed by Federal pursuit every step of the way.

On Saturday, October 30, the prisoners of the 2nd Kansas State Militia and their fellow prisoners were unexpectedly paroled. General Shelby, his adjutant Maj. John Edwards, and several clerks attempted to hold formal proceedings, but no sooner had they begun than the Federals under Pleasonton and A.J. Smith struck hard at the rear guard of the fleeing Southern army.

The prisoners were hastened under guard another two miles down the road toward Arkansas where, in a place of comparative safety to the Confederates, they swore "not to bear arms against the Southern Confederacy, or in any way contend against that government until duly exchanged." They then received parole papers and were left to their own devices.

Price at last realized that he could not escape with both his army and his huge wagon train. He ordered most of the wagons corralled and burned, and his army became a column of cavalry. Freed of the troublesome wagon train and the unmounted prisoners, the Rebels finally pulled ahead of Yankee troops. Once distanced from Pleasonton's volunteer and militia pursuers, Price felt safe enough to slow the pace of the retreat somewhat.

Price tried to put a good face on his invasion. He boasted that he had marched 1,400 miles, many more than any other

Confederate army. In reality, the campaign failed to achieve any of its important goals: it failed to ease the pressure on the Confederacy east of the Mississippi; it failed to secure military supplies from Missouri; most of the new recruits that joined the army had already deserted; though he started with about 12,000 men, he returned to Arkansas with fewer than 6,000; and the campaign failed to open the door to Kansas by the capture of either Fort Leavenworth or Fort Scott.

Organized Confederate resistance in Kansas and Missouri had come to an end. It seemed that there remained only the long months during which Kansas soldiers awaited their discharges.

But war continued to plague Kansans. The fighting wrecked many of the guerrilla bands and killed many of their leaders, including Bloody Bill Anderson, second in reputation only to Quantrill. Quantrill himself left the border, some said on his way east to assassinate President Lincoln, and was killed by Union militia in Kentucky. The few remaining bushwhackers went south with Price for the winter of 1864.

January 1865, witnessed a renewed fear of guerrilla raids. On January 31, the often-attacked village of Aubrey, Kansas, was again visited by bushwhackers, who burned what was left of the hamlet. A fortnight later, on February 15, 1865, a draft began in Kansas. For the first time during the war, the state's recruiters failed to fill the Federal government's quota of volunteers. This was the only time during the war that Kansans would be drafted.

By the time the war ended, Kansas had provided more troops to the war effort than actually lived in the state at any time during the war. A month later, on March 16, word spread rapidly that the draft was suspended. It was imposed partly to raise troops for the defense of the frontier, partly to restore law and order, and partly for the final push to defeat the Confederacy. Its suspension was cause for celebration and pride that the quota was filled so quickly.

While the War Between the States wound down, the war on

the frontier heated up. On February 1, 1865, Plains Indians attacked a squad of soldiers on wood-chopping detail out of Fort Zarah. Indian troubles along the Santa Fe Trail caused military posts to be garrisoned with volunteers from Iowa and Wisconsin as well as Kansas.

On February 11, a small detachment of cavalry scouts rode out as they had all winter from Fort Larned, only this time the snow was a foot deep and the temperature well below zero. Even though the woodcutting party from Fort Zarah had recently been attacked, the patrol reported all was quiet on the Indian frontier in that area.

Tensions on the southern plains mounted in spite of negotiations with the tribes. On April 10, 1865, Fort Dodge was established at a ford of the Arkansas River west of Fort Larned. Colonel Ford sent a short battalion under Capt.Henry Pearce and his Company C, 11th Kansas Volunteers, two companies of the 2nd U.S. Volunteer Infantry, and Company K of Ford's old regiment, the 2nd Colorado, to establish a post near where the Santa Fe Train split into two routes.

Further north along the Platte River Road in Nebraska Territory, Lt. Col. Preston B. Plumb led the 11th Kansas Volunteer Cavalry regiment—which had the fall before fought so hard against Price's invaders—out of Fort Riley up the Republican River to Fort Kearney, Nebraska, in February 1865. From there, companies of the regiment were parceled out along the Platte River Road and in Dakota Territory to protect that vital route from depredations by the Sioux.

The regiment's commander, Thomas Moonlight, joined his men later in the spring. By July 1865, some of the regiment fought again, this time not against Rebels but rather against red warriors at the desperate battle at Platte River Bridge Station.

In March 1865, Maj. Gen. Robert B. Mitchell of Kansas, who had defended the Nebraska frontier with a skeleton force of Iowa volunteers, was replaced so he could take command of the Department of Kansas at Fort Leavenworth.

The Indian war in Kansas flared up in April. On the 24th, Cheyenne attacked a wagon train on the Santa Fe Trail 15 miles east of Fort Zarah. Col. Jesse H. Leavenworth had made a trip south of the Arkansas River in March to open talks with Arapaho and Cheyenne leaders. Gen. Grenville M. Dodge, in command in the district, and Gen. Henry Halleck, in Washington, D.C., felt he was making progress.

They ordered a planned expedition against the hostiles under Coloradan Col. James Ford with some of his regiments and some Kansas troops delayed at Fort Zarah pending Leavenworth's talks. But the audacity of the attack on the wagon train sent a clear message that the war on the plains was imminent.

According to frontiersman Jesse Chisholm, who maintained a trading post near the modern city of Wichita and made frequent trading trips into the Nations, an Indian gathering at Fort Cobb, Indian Territory, had been addressed by a Confederate officer in the spring of 1865 with the intention of inciting the plains tribes.

While Federal officers pow wowed with hostiles, other Indian tribes experienced impacts from the war. James Abbott was agent to the Shawnee in Johnson County, Kansas, on the border with Missouri. He wrote to the U.S. commissioner of Indian affairs in Washington, D.C., on March 11, 1865, that Quantrill's raid on Lawrence had great effect on his wards.

Abbott had been in the Eldridge Hotel with $900 of tribal money when Quantrill attacked. Abbott's luggage, his carriage in the hotel's stable, and the wallet with the Shawnee money all appeared lost. However, he had dropped the wallet in a pig pen. The agent retrieved the badly chewed wallet and recovered all but $70 of the Shawnee money, but the Lawrence raid nearly cost the tribe most of its cash funds.

After Lee surrendered the Army of Northern Virginia at Appomattox, not only organized but also irregular resistance to Federal authority withered as other generals in the South surrendered. As word spread that the war was over, Kansans in most towns and cities in the state commemorated the end of the fighting with festivities. Then those same people who had a week before celebrated the fall of the Confederate capital of Richmond once more took to the streets back east.

President Lincoln had been posing for a 16-year-old Kansas girl, Vinnie Ream, who was preparing a sculpture of the great man. He had been sitting for her a half hour daily, but on April 14, 1865, he excused himself early to take his wife to the theater. Kansans grieved with the nation when Lincoln was shot that night.

Vinnie Ream's work with the president won her a competitive commission in 1866, when at age 18 she became the first woman, the first Kansan, and the youngest artist ever to be awarded such a Federal commission.

The day after President Lincoln died, newspapers such as the *Atchison Globe*, in which Col. John Martin, hero of the Battle of Chickamauga, wrote, were bordered with black in mourning. Buildings, too, were draped in black, businesses were closed, and people ecstatic only a week earlier at the news of Lee's surrender now gathered to speak in hushed tones. Gov. Samuel J. Crawford, late commander of the 2nd Kansas Colored Infantry, declared April 23 a statewide day of fasting and prayer. Churches held prayer services and towns arranged funeral processions for the martyred president.

Throughout the rest of 1865, Kansas regiments awaited orders to return to Kansas or to be mustered out. By the end of the year, the men had rejoined their families and returned to their farms or businesses. The Indian wars on the plains would continue for a decade. Some of the former guerrillas, such as Frank and Jesse James and the Younger brothers, turned outlaw to plague the border even longer. But as the outlawry and the hostile tribesmen were brought under control, often by the veterans of the Civil War in Kansas, the western two-thirds of the state filled with settlers, farms, ranches, railroads, and towns.

Today, as one crosses modern Kansas and surveys the quiet

and settled landscape, experiences the urban sprawl, and enjoys the general friendliness of the people, it is difficult to recall the bitter war that raged across the state and involved so many of its inhabitants both in the state and outside its borders so long ago. Many of the sites of these battles, raids, and skirmishes have vanished with time.

Still, there is practical value in remembering those cruel old days, an era far more violent than that of "bleeding Kansas" or any other of the state's time periods. It helps us understand how we got where we are today and where we are going to be in the future.

To this day, it defines Kansas and Kansans for what they are. Kansans can also draw inspiration when they need to draw on examples of courage and self-sacrifice of those who endured the trials and tribulations of the Civil War in the state.

Selected Bibliography

Ayres, Carol Dark. *Lincoln and Kansas: Partnership for Freedom.* Manhattan: Sunflower University Press, 2001.

Bearss, Edwin C. *The Battle of Wilson's Creek.* Cassville, MO: Wilson's Creek National Battlefield Foundation, 1992.

Bird, Roy. *Kansas Day By Day.* Tucson: The Patrice Press, 1996.

————. *They Deserved a Better Fate: The Second Kansas State Militia Regiment and the Price Raid, 1864.* New York: Cummings & Hathaway, 1998.

Britton, Wiley. *The Civil War on the Border.* (Two volumes.) New York: G.P. Putnam's Sons, 1899.

Brownlee, Richard S. *Gray Ghosts of the Confederacy: Guerrilla Warfare on the Western Border, 1861-1865.* Baton Rouge: Louisiana State University Press, 1958.

Castel, Albert. *Frontier State at War: Kansas, 1861-1865.* Ithaca: Cornell University Press.

Cornish, Dudley Taylor. *The Sable Arm: Negro Troops in the Union Army, 1863-1865.* New York: Longmans Green, 1956; reprint, W.W. Norton, 1966.

Crawford, Samuel J. *Kansas in the Sixties.* New York: A.C. McClurg & Co., 1911.

Dary, David. *Entrepreneurs of the Old West.* New York: Alfred A. Knopf, 1986.

Goodrich, Thomas. *Black Flag: Guerrilla Warfare on the Western*

Border, 1861-1865. Bloomington: Indiana University Press, 1995.

Miner, H. Craig and William C. Unrau. *The End of Indian Kansas: A Study of Cultural Revolution, 1854-1871*. Lawrence: Regents Press of Kansas, 1978.

Monaghan, Jay. *Civil War on the Western Border, 1854-1865*. Boston: Little, Brown and Company, 1955.

Nye, Wilbur S. *Plains Indian Raiders: The Final Phases of Warfare From the Arkansas to the Red River*. Norman: University of Oklahoma Press, 1968.

"Report of the Adjutant General of the State of Kansas." Volume I, 1861-1865. Leavenworth, 1867.

Richmond, Robert W. *Kansas: A Pictorial History*. Lawrence: University Press of Kansas, 1993.

Snell, Joseph G. "Famous and Infamous Women of Early Day Kansas." Unpublished Paper, n.p, n.d.

Spruill, Matt (ed.). *Guide to the Battle of Chickamauga*. Lawrence: University Press of Kansas, 1993.

Starr, Stephen S. *Jennison's Jawhawkers: A Civil War Cavalry Regiment and Its Commander*. Baton Rouge: Louisiana State University Press, 1973.

Ware, Eugene F. *The Indian War of 1864*. Topeka: Crane & Co., 1911; reprint, University of Nebraska Press, 1960.

West, Elliott. *Contested Plains: Indians, Goldseekers, and the Rush to Colorado*. Lawrence: University Press of Kansas, 1998.

Wilder, Daniel W. *Annuals of Kansas, 1541-1886*. Topeka: T. Dwight Thatcher, Kansas Publishing House, 1886.

APPENDIX

Index of Battles, Skirmishes, and Raids